Teach & Test

Language Grade 5

Table of Contents

How to Use This Book

1. This book can be used in a home or classroom setting. Read through each unit before working with the student(s). Familiarize yourself with the vocabulary and the skills that are introduced at the top of each unit activity page. Use this information as a guide to help instruct the student(s).

2. Choose a quiet place with little or no interruptions (including the telephone). Talk with the student(s) about the purpose of this book and how you will be working as a team to prepare for standardized tests.

3. As an option, copy the unit test and give it as a pretest to identify weak areas.

4. Upon the completion of each unit, you will find a unit test. Discuss the Helping Hand strategy for test taking featured on the test. Use the example on each test as a chance to show the student(s) how to work through a problem and completely fill in the answer circle. Encourage the student(s) to work independently when possible, but this is a learning time, and questions should be welcomed. A time limit is given for each test. Instruct the student(s) to use the time allowed efficiently, looking back over the answers if possible. Tell him to continue until he sees the stop sign.

5. Record the score on the record sheet on page 4. If a student has difficulty with any questions, use the cross-reference guide on the inside back cover to identify the skills that need to be reviewed.

Introduction

Now this makes sense—teaching students the skills and strategies that are expected of them before they are tested!

Many students, parents, and teachers are concerned that standardized test scores do not adequately reflect a child's capabilities. This may be due to one or more of the factors italicized below. The purpose of this book is to reduce the negative impact of these, or similar factors, on a student's standardized test scores. The goal is to target those factors and alter their effects as described.

1. *The student has been taught the tested skills but has forgotten them.* This book is divided into units that are organized similarly to fifth grade textbooks. Instructions for the skill itself are found at the top of each unit activity page, ensuring that the student has been exposed to each key component. The exercises include drill/practice and creative learning activities. Additional activity suggestions can be found in a star burst within the units. These activities require the students to apply the skills that they are practicing.

2. *The student has mastered the skills but has never seen them presented in a test-type format.* Ideally, the skills a student learns at school will be used as part of problem solving in the outside world. For this reason, the skills in this book, and in most classrooms, are not practiced in a test-type format. At the end of each unit in this book, the skills are specifically matched with test questions. In this way, the book serves as a type of "bridge" between the skills that the student(s) has mastered and the standardized test format.

3. *The student is inexperienced with the answer sheet format.* Depending on the standardized test that your school district uses, students are expected to fill in the answer circles completely and neatly. The unit, midway review, and final review tests will help prepare the student(s) for this process.

4. *The student may feel the anxiety of a new and unfamiliar situation.* While testing, students will notice changes in their daily routine: their classroom door will be closed with a "Testing" sign on it, they will be asked not to use the restroom, their desks may be separated, their teacher may read from a script and refuse to repeat herself, etc. To help relieve the stress caused by these changes, treat each unit test in this book as it would be treated at school by following the procedures listed below.

Stage a Test

You will find review tests midway through the book and again at the end of the book. When you reach these points, "stage a test" by creating a real test-taking environment. The procedures listed below coincide with many standardized test directions. The purpose is to alleviate stress, rather than contribute to it, so make this a serious, but calm, event and the student(s) will benefit.

1. Prepare! Have the student(s) sharpen two pencils, lay out scratch paper, and use the restroom.

2. Choose a room with a door that can be closed. Ask a student to put a sign on the door that reads "Testing" and explain that no talking will be permitted after the sign is hung.

3. Direct the student(s) to turn to a specific page but not to begin until the instructions are completely given.

4. Read the instructions at the top of the page and work through the example together. Discuss the Helping Hand strategy that is featured at the top of the page. Have the student(s) neatly and completely fill in the bubble for the example. This is the child's last chance to ask for help!

5. Instruct the student(s) to continue working until the stop sign is reached. If a student needs help reading, you may read each question only once.

Helping Hand Test Strategies

The first page of each test features a specific test-taking strategy that will be helpful in working through most standardized tests. These strategies are introduced and spotlighted one at a time so that they will be learned and remembered internally. Each will serve as a valuable test-taking tool, so discuss them thoroughly.

The strategies include:

- Sometimes the correct answer is not given. Fill in the circle beside NG if no answer is correct.
- Always read each question carefully.
- Fill in the answer circles completely and neatly.
- Read all the answer choices before you choose the one you think is correct.
- Cross out answers you know are wrong.
- Use your time wisely. If a question seems too tough, skip it and come back to it later.
- Take time to review your answers.

Constructed-Response Questions

You will find the final question of each test is written in a different format called constructed response. This means that students are not provided with answer choices, but are instead asked to construct their own answers. The objective of such an "open-ended" type of question is to provide students with a chance to creatively develop reasonable answers. It also provides an insight to a student's reasoning and thinking skills. As this format is becoming more accepted and encouraged by standardized test developers, students will be "ahead of the game" by practicing such responses now.

Evaluating the Tests

Two types of questions are included in each test. The unit tests and the midway review test each consist of 20 multiple-choice questions, and the final review test consists of 30 multiple-choice questions. All tests include a constructed-response question which requires the student(s) to construct and sometimes support an answer. Use the following procedures to evaluate a student's performance on each test.

1. Use the answer key found on pages 124–128 to correct the tests. Be sure the student(s) neatly and completely filled in the answer circles.

2. Record the scores on the record sheet found on page 4. If the student(s) incorrectly answered any questions, use the cross-reference guide found on the inside back cover to help identify the skills the student(s) needs to review. Each test question references the corresponding activity page.

3. Scoring the constructed response questions is somewhat subjective. Discuss these questions with the student(s). Sometimes it is easier for the student(s) to explain the answer verbally. Help the student to record her thoughts as a written answer. If the student(s) has difficulty formulating a response, refer back to the activity pages using the cross-reference guide. Also review the star burst activity found in the unit which also requires the student(s) to formulate an answer.

4. Discuss the test with the student(s). What strategies were used to answer the questions? Were some questions more difficult than others? Was there enough time? What strategies did the student(s) use while taking the test?

Record Sheet

Record a student's score for each test by drawing a star or placing a sticker below each item number that was correct. Leave the incorrect boxes empty as this will allow you to visually see any weak spots. Review and practice those missed skills, then retest only the necessary items.

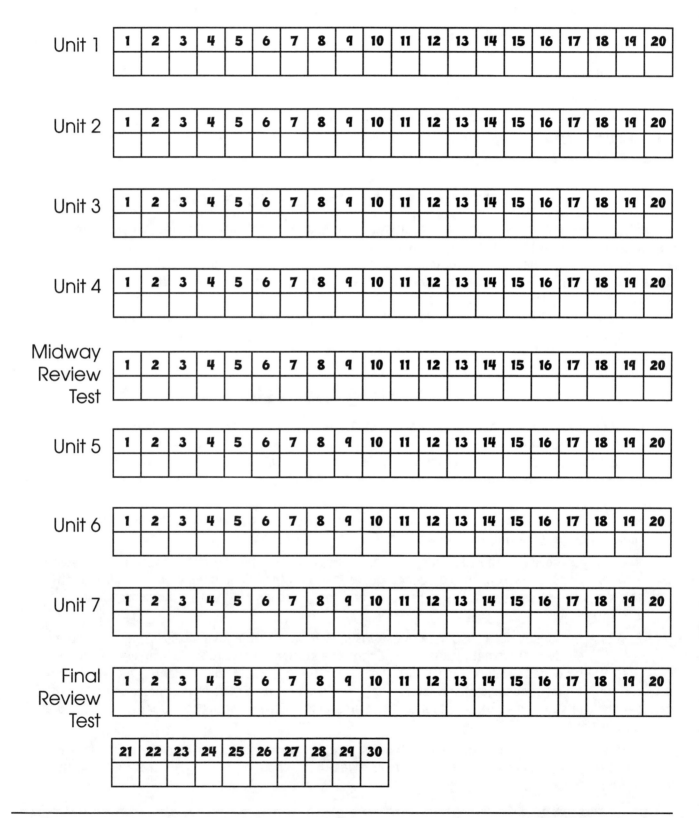

	1	2	3	4	5	6	7	8	9	10	11	12	13	14	15	16	17	18	19	20
Unit 1																				

	1	2	3	4	5	6	7	8	9	10	11	12	13	14	15	16	17	18	19	20
Unit 2																				

	1	2	3	4	5	6	7	8	9	10	11	12	13	14	15	16	17	18	19	20
Unit 3																				

	1	2	3	4	5	6	7	8	9	10	11	12	13	14	15	16	17	18	19	20
Unit 4																				

	1	2	3	4	5	6	7	8	9	10	11	12	13	14	15	16	17	18	19	20
Midway Review Test																				

	1	2	3	4	5	6	7	8	9	10	11	12	13	14	15	16	17	18	19	20
Unit 5																				

	1	2	3	4	5	6	7	8	9	10	11	12	13	14	15	16	17	18	19	20
Unit 6																				

	1	2	3	4	5	6	7	8	9	10	11	12	13	14	15	16	17	18	19	20
Unit 7																				

	1	2	3	4	5	6	7	8	9	10	11	12	13	14	15	16	17	18	19	20
Final Review Test																				

21	22	23	24	25	26	27	28	29	30

Name

Concrete and abstract nouns

A **common concrete noun** is a word that names any person, place, or thing. A concrete noun identifies someone or something that can be seen, heard, smelled, touched, or tasted.
Examples: <u>actor</u> (person), <u>theater</u> (place), <u>play</u> (thing)

An **abstract noun** is a word that names an idea or quality that has no physical existence.
Examples: <u>suggestion</u> (idea), <u>kindness</u> (quality)

Concrete or Abstract?

Write the concrete nouns in the Word Bank under the correct headings.

spinster	mansion	awning	lobby	fortress	bachelor
pharmacy	cabinet	infant	orphan	souvenir	university
maiden	studio	hexagon	table	partner	satellite

Persons	**Places**	**Things**
_____	_____	_____
_____	_____	_____
_____	_____	_____
_____	_____	_____
_____	_____	_____
_____	_____	_____

Write **concrete** or **abstract** to identify each of the common nouns below.

1. revenge _____

2. bravery _____

3. textile _____

4. imagination _____

5. sympathy _____

6. freedom _____

7. detour _____

8. gratitude _____

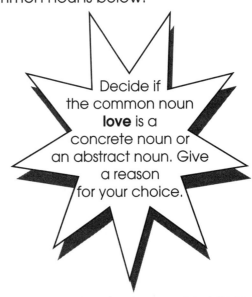

Decide if the common noun **love** is a concrete noun or an abstract noun. Give a reason for your choice.

Name _____

Proper nouns

A **proper noun** names a special person, place, or thing. It begins with a capital letter.
A proper noun may be more than one word.
Examples: <u>Neil Armstrong</u> (special person), <u>Earth</u> (special place), and <u>*Apollo 11*</u> (special thing)

Space Race!

Underline the proper nouns in the sentences.

1. The Soviets launched *Sputnik I*, the first satellite, into space in 1957.

2. Then they launched a satellite carrying a dog named Laika.

3. Next, they sent an unmanned spaceship to the moon.

4. Yuri Gagarin of the Soviet Union was the first person to travel in space.

5. Then President Kennedy of the United States made space exploration a priority.

6. John Glenn, an astronaut in the *Mercury* program, orbited Earth in 1962.

7. The *Apollo 11* mission to the moon was successful in 1969.

8. The command module was called the *Columbia*.

9. The lunar module carried Neil Armstrong and "Buzz" Aldrin.

10. It was called the *Eagle*, and the whole world watched it land on the moon.

11. The astronauts were spoken to from the White House.

12. The astronauts returned safely and were given a huge parade in New York City.

13. The race to send a human to the moon was won by the United States!

Write the underlined words under the correct headings. Do not use a proper noun more than once.

People	Places	Things
_____	_____	_____
_____	_____	_____
_____	_____	_____
_____	_____	_____
_____	_____	_____
	_____	_____

Name _____

Identifying singular, plural, and collective nouns   Unit 1

A **singular noun** names one person, place, thing, or idea. Example: The <u>boy</u> plays softball.

A **plural noun** names more than one person, place, thing, or idea. It often ends in **-s** or **-es**. Example: The <u>boys</u> play on a team.

A **collective noun** names a group of persons or things. It is considered a singular noun in a sentence if the word is used as a unit. Example: The <u>team</u> is in first place. (*Is* is a singular verb.)

A Collection of Nouns

Identify the common nouns. Write **S** for singular, **P** for plural, and **C** for collective.

_____ 1. audience   _____ 2. crowd   _____ 3. government

_____ 4. biscuits   _____ 5. icicle   _____ 6. valley

_____ 7. errand   _____ 8. committee   _____ 9. flock

_____ 10. crew   _____ 11. sandwiches   _____ 12. stack

_____ 13. hydrants   _____ 14. morsel   _____ 15. family

Write the collective noun from the Word Bank that names each group of animals. Refer to a dictionary if needed.

pack	litter	swarm	plague
gaggle	herd	school	pod

16. _____ of puppies   17. _____ of bees

18. _____ of geese   19. _____ of locusts

20. _____ of whales   21. _____ of fish

22. _____ of elephants   23. _____ of wolves

Write a sentence for each collective noun: slate (of candidates), field (of runners), fleet (of ships).

24. _____

25. _____

26. _____

Name

Making nouns plural

A **plural noun** names more than one person, place, thing, or idea.

Add **-s** to most singular nouns to make them plural. Example: book/book_s_

If a singular noun ends with **sh**, **ch**, **x**, **s**, or **z**, add **-es** to make it plural.
Example: beach/beach_es_

If a singular noun ends with a consonant followed by **-y**, change the **-y** to **-i**, and add
-es to make the word plural. Example: baby/bab_ies_

If the singular noun ends with a vowel followed by **-y**, just add **-s** to make the plural.
Example: boy/boy_s_

Easter Island Mystery

Write the plural of each singular noun.

1. crash _____

2. comic _____

3. lady _____

4. dentist _____

5. suggestion _____

6. decision _____

7. address _____

8. branch _____

9. glimpse _____

10. responsibility _____

11. buzz _____

12. tax _____

13. princess _____

14. display _____

15. tortilla _____

16. melody _____

Complete each sentence with the plural of the noun in parentheses.

17. Many people are interested in ancient _____. (mystery)

18. One mystery concerns gigantic stone _____ on Easter Island. (statue)

19. The stone _____ were all carved inside an extinct volcano. (figure)

20. Scientists wonder how the _____ could have moved the 30-ton pieces
    from the quarry to other positions on the island. (islander)

21. They all look alike with deep eye sockets that have no _____. (eye)

22. Their _____ are long, and their chins are pointed. (earlobe)

23. They are thought to have been funeral _____. (monument)

24. The _____ of the dead were laid to rest on the stone platforms. (body)

Name _____

Making nouns plural

Some singular nouns that end in **-f** or **-fe** are made plural by adding **-s**.
Example: roof/roof<u>s</u>

Some singular nouns that end in **-f** or **-fe** are made plural by changing the **-f** or **-fe** to **-v** and adding **-es**. Example: scarf/scar<u>ves</u>

Some singular nouns end with a consonant letter followed by **-o**. Add **-es** to form the plural. Example: hero/hero<u>es</u> (Note: There are exceptions like photo/photo<u>s</u>.)

Some singular nouns end with a vowel letter followed by **-o**. Add **-s** to form the plural. Example: scenario/scenario<u>s</u>

Some singular nouns have irregular forms, and others do not change to form plurals. These exceptions to the rules for making nouns plural must be learned.

Stolen Property

Write the plural of each singular noun. Check a dictionary, as there are exceptions to some rules.

1. sheep _____
2. loaf _____
3. knife _____
4. life _____
5. ox _____
6. mouse _____
7. echo _____
8. rodeo _____
9. leaf _____
10. belief _____
11. tooth _____
12. half _____
13. wolf _____
14. tomato _____
15. volcano _____
16. piano _____

Complete each sentence with the plural of the singular noun in parentheses.

17. Two police officers were looking for jewel _____. (thief)

18. Some _____ had been robbed of valuable jewelry. (woman)

19. One lady was missing several expensive _____. (cameo)

20. The officers showed her two _____ of suspects. (photo)

21. She identified one of the _____ as someone she had seen before. (man)

22. The officers suggested that the ladies keep their jewelry in _____. (safe)

Name _____

Possessive nouns

A **possessive noun** is a word that shows who or what has something or owns something. Add an apostrophe and **-s** (**'s**) to most singular common and proper nouns to show possession. Examples: girl/girl's, Olivia/Olivia's

Add an apostrophe (') to most plural common and proper nouns to show possession. Examples: mountains/mountains', Alps/Alps'

Add an apostrophe and **-s** (**'s**) to most irregular plural nouns to show possession. Example: women/women's

Impressive Possessives

Write the possessive form of each noun.

1. berries _____

2. teeth _____

3. bracelet _____

4. galaxy _____

5. men _____

6. T-rex _____

7. Tess _____

8. children _____

9. industries _____

10. sausages _____

11. meadow _____

12. tennis _____

13. Tuesday _____

14. countesses _____

15. Howard _____

16. melon _____

Rewrite each phrase below using a possessive noun for each underlined noun. Follow the example.

Example: the shoe belonging to <u>Mel</u>/Mel's shoe

17. the flavor of the <u>French fries</u> _____

18. the economy of <u>Canada</u> _____

19. the cheers of the <u>crowd</u> _____

20. the aroma of the <u>pies</u> _____

21. the displays of the <u>museum</u> _____

22. the flight of the <u>astronauts</u> _____

23. the creations of the <u>artist</u> _____

24. the dreams of the <u>immigrants</u> _____

Name _____

Subject pronouns Unit 1

You and **I** are pronouns that can be used as the subject of a sentence. They can stand alone. No reference is needed to the noun or phrase these pronouns are replacing. Example: <u>You</u> and <u>I</u> are learning about bats.

He, she, it, we, and **they** are also **subject pronouns** that can replace nouns and phrases containing nouns in the subject of a sentence. Example: <u>Bats</u> are mammals that can fly. <u>They</u> are mammals that can fly.

Batty About Bats!

Write **he, she, it, we,** or **they** to replace the words below.

1. scientists _____   2. caves _____

3. Robert _____   4. research _____

5. you and I _____   6. Tina _____

Rewrite the sentences substituting subject pronouns for the underlined words.

7. <u>Tina and Robert</u> visited Dr. Alex Tran to learn about bats.

_____

8. <u>Dr. Tran</u> explained that hearing is very important to bats.

_____

9. <u>Bats</u> have large ears with ridges and folds of skin.

_____

10. <u>A bat</u> makes sounds and listens for their echoes.

_____

11. <u>The echoes</u> enable the bat to locate objects in the dark.

_____

12. <u>Tina</u> asked Dr. Tran how bats make sounds.

_____

13. <u>Dr. Tran</u> said some bats make sounds through their mouths.

_____

14. <u>Other bats</u> make sounds through their noses.

_____

© Carson-Dellosa CD-4314   **11**   Teach & Test Language: Grade 5

Name _____

Unit 1

Object pronouns

Object pronouns are used in the predicate of a sentence. They receive the action of the verb.
You and **me** are object pronouns that don't need a reference to the noun or phrase these pronouns are replacing.
Example: Mr. Vogel told <u>you</u> and <u>me</u> about Captain James Cook.

Him, her, it, us, and **them** are object pronouns.
Example: Captain Cook left <u>Britain</u> in 1768. Captain Cook left <u>it</u> in 1768.

Courageous Captain Cook

Write **him, her, it, us**, or **them** to replace the words below.

1. Australia _____

2. islands _____

3. you and me _____

4. exploration _____

5. sailors _____

6. maps _____

7. voyages _____

8. Pacific Ocean _____

9. ship _____

10. scientists _____

Rewrite the sentences substituting object pronouns for the underlined words.

11. Captain Cook landed on <u>Tahiti, a Pacific island</u>, in 1769.

_____

12. Scientists on the voyage made <u>observations of Venus</u> from the island.

_____

13. Later Cook's ship, the *Endeavor*, took <u>Cook</u> to New Zealand.

_____

14. He was the first European to visit <u>New Zealand</u>.

_____

15. On his second voyage, Cook circled Antarctica and visited <u>more islands</u>.

_____

16. Cook's final voyage took <u>the captain</u> to the Hawaiian Islands.

_____

17. Mr. Vogel told <u>you and me</u> that Captain Cook was a great explorer.

_____

Subject and object pronouns   Unit 1

He, she, it, we, and **they** are **subject pronouns** that can replace nouns and phrases containing nouns in the subject of a sentence. **You** and **I** are subject pronouns that don't need a reference to the noun or phrase these pronouns are replacing.

Examples: <u>Robert Browning</u> was a poet. <u>He</u> was a poet. <u>You</u> and <u>I</u> enjoy his poetry.

Object pronouns are used in the predicate of a sentence. They receive the action of the verb. **Him, her, it, us,** and **them** are object pronouns. **You** and **me** are object pronouns that don't need a reference to the noun or phrase these pronouns are replacing.

Examples: Robert Browning married <u>Elizabeth Barrett</u> in 1846. Robert Browning married <u>her</u> in 1846. Mother reads the Brownings' poetry to <u>you</u> and <u>me</u>.

Some sentences have two subject parts or two nouns or phrases in the predicate. Subject and object pronouns can replace them. Example: <u>Robert</u> and <u>Elizabeth Browning</u> were poets. <u>He</u> and <u>she</u> were poets.

A Pair of Poets

Rewrite each sentence using subject or object pronouns for the underlined words or phrases.

1. <u>Robert Browning</u> was born in Camberwell, England, in 1812.

   _____

   _____

2. Robert was interested in writing about <u>people of the past</u>.

   _____

3. <u>Elizabeth Barrett</u> was a poet during the Victorian period in England.

   _____

4. Her health was poor, and she spent most of her time writing <u>poetry</u> in her room.

   _____

5. Robert admired <u>her poetry</u>, and he wrote <u>Elizabeth</u>.

   _____

6. <u>Robert</u> and <u>Elizabeth</u> met and fell in love.

   _____

7. <u>Elizabeth's father</u> disapproved of their marriage and never forgave <u>Elizabeth</u>.

   _____

8. They left England, and Italy became the home of <u>Robert</u> and <u>Elizabeth</u>.

   _____

Name _____

Possessive pronouns

My, your, her, his, its, our, and **their** are **possessive pronouns** that show who or what has something or owns something. Use these possessive pronouns in front of nouns. Example: _My brother_ and I enjoy foreign travel.

Our, your, and **their** are **plural possessive pronouns**.
Example: _Our trip_ to Morocco was outstanding.

Mine, yours, his, and **hers** are **singular possessive pronouns** that don't need a reference to the noun or phrase these pronouns are replacing.
Example: These photographs of the trip are <u>his</u> and <u>mine</u>.

Ours, yours, and **theirs** are **plural possessive pronouns** that don't need a reference to the noun or phrase these pronouns are replacing.
Example: <u>Ours</u> are very similar photographs.

The Road to Morocco

Rewrite each sentence substituting a possessive pronoun for the underlined words.

1. <u>Volubilis's</u> ruins can be seen on a high plateau in Morocco.

   _____

2. They are what remain of <u>the ancient Romans'</u> city.

   _____

3. <u>My brother's</u> guidebook said Volubilis had 40 towers and seven gates.

   _____

4. <u>My pictures</u> show the main street, Decumanus Maximus.

   _____

5. Some of <u>the street's</u> houses still contain beautiful mosaics.

   _____

6. A marble arch built in <u>the Emperor Caracalla's</u> honor still stands.

   _____

7. Volubilis is now one of <u>Morocco's</u> World Heritage Sites.

   _____

8. I hope <u>your next vacation</u> can be to Morocco and Volubilis.

   _____

9. <u>My next trip</u> will be to Cairo.

   _____

Name _____

Reflexive pronouns

Myself, yourself, itself, herself, and **himself** are **singular reflexive pronouns**.
Reflexive pronouns reflect the action of the verb back to the subject.
Example: Leonardo da Vinci painted with a style that made the painting <u>itself</u> look misty.

Ourselves, yourselves, and **themselves** are **plural reflexive pronouns**.
Example: All of you can see the painting's soft and muted colors for <u>yourselves</u>.

Reflect on da Vinci

Identify the reflexive pronoun in each sentence.
Write it on the line.

1. The woman in Leonardo da Vinci's painting,
   the *Mona Lisa*, seems to be smiling to herself. _____

2. For centuries, people have asked themselves why this
   is so. _____

3. I have wondered myself about her mysterious smile. _____

4. Leonardo da Vinci kept that secret to himself. _____

5. If you want to see the *Mona Lisa* yourself, go to the Louvre in Paris. _____

Complete each sentence with the correct pronoun in parentheses.

6. Leonardo developed a new painting technique _____. (itself, himself)

7. He used it to apply paint directly to a wall _____. (themselves, itself)

8. Leonardo da Vinci painted Jesus sitting at a table with his disciples, who were
   arguing among _____. (himself, themselves)

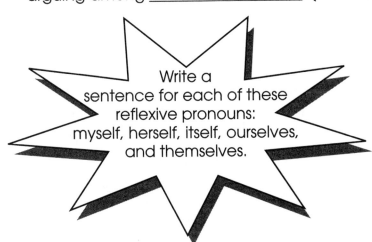

Write a sentence for each of these reflexive pronouns: myself, herself, itself, ourselves, and themselves.

9. Unfortunately, the fresco's paint
   began to flake and fade by
   _____ after a few
   years. (myself, itself)

10. We can see *The Last Supper*,
    which has been restored, for
    _____ in Milan.
    (yourselves, ourselves)

Interrogative and demonstrative pronouns

An **interrogative pronoun** introduces a question. **Who, which,** and **what** are interrogative pronouns. *Whom* and *whose* are forms of *who*.

Examples: <u>Who</u> is he? <u>Whom</u> do you see? <u>Whose</u> is this? (Do not confuse *whose* with the contraction *who's*.) <u>Which</u> of you can help me? <u>What</u> is the answer?

This and **that** are singular **demonstrative pronouns** that refer to a particular thing or action. **These** and **those** are the plural forms.

Examples: <u>This</u> is nice. <u>That</u> is nicer. <u>These</u> are fine. <u>Those</u> are finer. (Be careful: *this, that, these,* and *those* can also be used as adjectives and adverbs.)

Prehistoric People

Complete each sentence with the correct pronoun in parentheses.

1. Prehistoric people did not have writing. _____ is a fact. (This, These)

2. The first writing was pictograms. _____ are little pictures. (That, Those)

3. _____ is the importance of pictograms? (What, Which)

4. The pictograms tell us about prehistoric people. _____ tell us about how they lived and about their beliefs. (This, These)

5. _____ were some of their beliefs? (Whom, What)

6. Some Australian Aborigines believed in spirit-beings responsible for rain and storms.

   _____ is very interesting. (Those, That)

7. Some prehistoric people believed that art was a form of magic. _____ might find that strange today? (That, Who)

8. _____ were some of the earliest paintings found in France? (Who, What)

9. _____ would be handprints made about 18,000 B.C. (Those, Whose)

10. _____ is true? (Which, Whose)

On another sheet of paper, write a sentence for each pronoun: who, what, this, these.

Name _____

Read or listen to the directions. Fill in the circle beside the best answer.

☐ Example:

Which word is not a common noun?

(A) discipline

(B) Sahara

(C) sponge

(D) NG

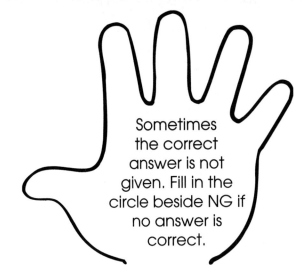

Sometimes the correct answer is not given. Fill in the circle beside NG if no answer is correct.

Answer: B because it names a special place and begins with a capital letter.

Now try these. You have 20 minutes. Continue until you see ⬡STOP⬡.

---

1. Which words are the common concrete nouns in the following sentence?

   Laney set the table with the finest china and crystal.

   (A) set, table, finest
   (B) table, finest, china
   (C) table, china, crystal
   (D) Laney, table, crystal

---

2. Which word is not an abstract noun?

   pleasure   strength   weakness   necklace
   (A)   (B)   (C)   (D)

---

3. Which sentence has an abstract noun?

   (A) Ludwig van Beethoven learned to play the violin and piano from his father.
   (B) He became a great composer.
   (C) He wrote nine symphonies.
   (D) He had the courage to continue composing after he became deaf.

GO ON

Name

4. What are the proper nouns in the following sentence?

People from Europe began settling in Australia and New Zealand in the 1700's.

(A) People, Europe, settling

(B) Europe, Australia, New Zealand

(C) People, Australia, New Zealand

(D) Australia, New Zealand, 1700's

Which words are not singular nouns in 5 and 6?

5.

secretary (A)

editor (B)

principals (C)

manuscript (D)

6.

lattice (A)

morsels (B)

polygon (C)

cycle (D)

---

7. Which word is a collective noun in the sentence?

A pack of hungry wolves attacked an injured deer.

pack (A)

injured (B)

wolves (C)

deer (D)

---

8. Which word is not a collective noun?

choir (A)

legislature (B)

swarm (C)

locusts (D)

---

9. Which sentence does not have a plural noun?

(A) The Sahara Desert is among the least populated places on Earth.

(B) People still travel across the desert in camel caravans.

(C) They are often searching for plants to feed their sheep and goats.

(D) The climate makes the Sahara a harsh place to live.

---

10. Which word is the correct plural form of **mystery**?

mysteries (A)

mysterys (B)

mystery's (C)

NG (D)

GO ON

Unit 1 Test

11. Which plural is not written correctly?

leaves
(A)

shelves
(B)

studios
(C)

patioes
(D)

Choose the correct possessive form of the nouns in 12 and 13.

12. raspberry

raspberries
(A)

raspberry's
(B)

raspberrys'
(C)

raspberrie's
(D)

13. Jess

Jesse's
(A)

Jes's
(B)

Jessie's
(C)

NG
(D)

Choose the correct pronoun for the underlined words in 14 and 15.

14. <u>Virgil and Tyler</u> climbed the rocky hill.

They
(A)

Them
(B)

Their
(C)

We
(D)

15. Rain forests are being cut down all over <u>the world</u>.

them
(A)

it
(B)

theirs
(C)

you
(D)

16. Which pronoun completes the sentence correctly?

The actor reviewed _____ script before the rehearsal.

mine
(A)

ours
(B)

his
(C)

its
(D)

17. Which pronouns can replace the underlined proper nouns?

The basset hound belongs to <u>Lowell</u> and <u>Lisa</u>.

he and she
(A)

his and her
(B)

him and her
(C)

him and she
(D)

GO ON

18. Which word is not a possessive pronoun?

My brother and I took our game board to his room.

My
(A)

I
(B)

our
(C)

his
(D)

19. Which reflexive pronoun can complete the sentence correctly?

My mom can fix the washing machine _____.

myself
(A)

ourselves
(B)

herself
(C)

itself
(D)

20. Which pronoun can complete the sentence correctly?

_____ is the best apple pie I have ever eaten.

Those
(A)

This
(B)

These
(C)

Who
(D)

Write a sentence with a proper noun and a collective noun. Then rewrite the sentence using pronouns.

_____

_____

_____

STOP

Name

Present tense action verbs   Unit 2

A **present tense action verb** shows action that is happening now. Present tense action
verbs end in **–s** or **–es** when the noun in the subject of a sentence is singular.
Examples: A piranha <u>attacks</u> fish.

Ferocious Fish!

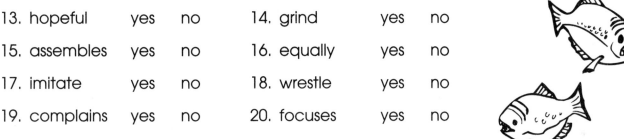

Are the words action verbs? Circle yes or no for each correct answer.

1. summarize yes no	2. cruises yes no
3. glide yes no	4. illustrates yes no
5. pathway yes no	6. opposite yes no
7. erase yes no	8. discusses yes no
9. preach yes no	10. stumbles yes no
11. cheery yes no	12. spectacles yes no
13. hopeful yes no	14. grind yes no
15. assembles yes no	16. equally yes no
17. imitate yes no	18. wrestle yes no
19. complains yes no	20. focuses yes no

Underline the action verb in each sentence. Write it on the line.

21. Clusters of plants float near a South American riverbank. _____

22. A piranha hatches from an egg on a water plant. _____

23. It hides among the plant's stems and roots. _____

24. The plants protect the tiny piranha from predators. _____

25. It swims slowly through the tangle of plants. _____

26. The little fish searches for crustaceans and insects to eat. _____

27. Most adult piranhas eat fish. _____

28. They use their razor-sharp teeth to bite pieces off their prey. _____

29. Piranhas swallow chunks of food whole. _____

30. Some piranhas scavenge dead animals and people. _____

Name _____

Present tense action verbs and linking verbs

A **present tense action verb** shows action that is happening now. Present tense action verbs end in **-s** or **-es** when the noun in the subject is singular.
Example: A young boy <u>plays</u> in the courtyard of his home in Pompeii, Italy.

A **linking verb** does not show action. It links the subject of a sentence to a noun or adjective in the predicate. Present tense forms of the verb **be**—*am, is, are*—and the verb **have**—*have, has*—are common linking verbs. *Appear, become, feel, look, seem, smell, taste,* and *turn* can also be used as linking verbs.
Example: The day <u>is</u> August 24, 79 A.D.

Vesuvius, the Violent Volcano

Identify each word as an action verb-**A**, a linking verb-**L**, or neither one-**N**.

1. seems _____   2. extinct _____

3. crashes _____   4. escape _____

5. feels _____   6. floats _____

7. shake _____   8. thirty _____

9. surrenders _____   10. become _____

Write the present tense action verbs or linking verbs in parentheses in the blanks.

11. The day _____ as any other day in Pompeii. (begins, began)

12. Children play, and shopkeepers _____ their goods. (sell, sold)

13. People _____ at the Forum to discuss current events. (gather, gathered)

14. Suddenly, at midday, Mount Vesuvius _____. (exploded, explodes)

15. Stones, pumice, and ash _____ 12 miles into the air. (shot, shoot)

16. The 20,000 people in Pompeii _____ in every direction. (dashed, dash)

17. Hot ash and pumice _____ down on the city. (rain, rained)

18. Some people _____ this disaster by boat. (escaped, escape)

19. Others _____ safe by riding horses and mules out of the city.
    (were, are)

20. Two feet of ash _____ Pompeii within hours of the eruption.
    (covered, cover)

Name _____

Past tense action verbs

A **past tense action verb** shows action that has already happened. The past tense
of most action verbs is made by adding **–ed** to the present tense verb.
Example: talk/talk<u>ed</u>

However, if the verb ends in silent **–e**, drop the **–e** and add **–ed**. Example: smile/smil<u>ed</u>

If the verb ends with a single consonant preceded by a single vowel, double the
consonant and add **–ed**. Example: flap/flap<u>ped</u>

If the verb ends in a consonant letter and **–y**, change the **–y** to **–i** and add **–ed** to write
the past tense. Example: study/stud<u>ied</u>

Pony Rider

Write the past tense of each present tense action verb.

1. delay _____   2. help _____

3. place _____   4. arrive _____

5. slip _____   6. trim _____

7. magnify _____   8. propel _____

Write the past tense of the present tense verb
in parentheses to complete each sentence.

9. In 1860, Hank _____ a help-wanted ad in the newspaper. (answer)

10. The sixteen-year old boy _____ to be a Pony Express rider. (want)

11. He _____ and was accepted for the extremely dangerous job. (apply)

12. As a Pony Express rider, Hank _____ the United States mail between
    "swing" stations that were 50 to 100 miles apart. (carry)

13. "Relay" stations between "swing" stations
    _____ him with fresh horses. (supply)

14. Hank _____ the mail pouch to the
    next rider waiting at the "swing" station. (pass)

15. The mail route _____ through
    1,800 miles of western wilderness. (stretch)

16. Pony riders _____ the mail in just 10 days from
    St. Joseph, Missouri, to Sacramento, California. (deliver)

Name

Past tense action verbs and linking verbs

Past tense action verbs show action that has already happened.
Example: The chameleon <u>climbed</u> the tree.

Linking verbs do not show action. They link the subject of a sentence to a noun or adjective in the predicate. The past tense forms of the linking verb **be** are *was* and *were*. The past tense of the linking verb **have** is *had*. Example: The chameleon <u>had</u> scales on its body. (*Had* links the noun in the subject to the noun in the predicate.)

The Changing Chameleon

Underline the past tense action verbs and linking verbs. Then write **A** for action or **L** for linking on the lines.

_____ 1. The chameleon had two big bulging eyes on either side of its head.

_____ 2. It rotated its eyes in two different directions.

_____ 3. The chameleon's feet were unusual, also.

_____ 4. Each foot had two bunches of toes with claws.

_____ 5. The claws helped the chameleon cling to the tree.

_____ 6. It wrapped its prehensile tail around a branch.

_____ 7. The chameleon waited patiently for an unsuspecting insect.

_____ 8. Then it spotted a grasshopper.

_____ 9. The chameleon's long tongue exploded out of its mouth.

_____ 10. The grasshopper struggled in the sticky mucus on the chameleon's tongue.

_____ 11. The chameleon pulled the insect into its mouth.

_____ 12. It chewed up the grasshopper with its tiny teeth.

Complete each sentence with the past tense verb in parentheses. Write it in the blank.

13. The chameleon _____ the ability to change colors. (had, has)

14. The chameleon's colors _____ its mood and environment. (reflected, reflect)

15. When the reptile _____ afraid, its color rapidly became darker. (is, was)

16. The color of its stripes _____ that it was in a fighting mood. (show, showed)

17. When the danger was over, the chameleon _____ to a lighter color. (changed, change)

Name

Present, past, and future tense verbs

A **present tense action verb** tells about an action that is happening now. A **present tense linking verb** tells what the subject of a sentence is or is like. Examples: Companies <u>develop</u> new medicines from plants. Plants <u>are</u> a source of medicines.

A **past tense action verb** tells about an action that has already happened. A **past tense linking verb** tells what the subject of a sentence was or was like. Examples: People <u>discovered</u> many plants could cure illnesses. Early herbalists <u>were</u> medical pioneers.

A **future tense verb** tells about an action that will happen in the future. Use *will* with a verb to form the future tense. Example: People <u>will continue</u> to search for new medicines.

Medicinal Plants

Fill in the chart with the present, past, and/or future tenses of each verb.

Present	Past	Future
1. hurry	_____	_____
2. _____	_____	will browse
3. _____	argued	_____
4. lecture	_____	_____
5. _____	criticized	_____
6. _____	_____	will promote

Identify the underlined verbs. Write **present**, **past**, or **future** on the line.

7. Apothecaries <u>were</u> the pharmacies of the Middle Ages. _____

8. The apothecary <u>dispensed</u> medicines from herbs and dried plants. _____

9. The apothecary <u>measured</u> the dosage carefully. _____

10. Unfortunately, he <u>was</u> uncertain of just what the right dosage should be. _____

11. Today's pharmacists <u>fill</u> prescriptions written by doctors for their patients. _____

12. Many drugs <u>contain</u> plant ingredients. _____

13. Foxglove <u>is</u> a very important plant for heart patients. _____

14. Digitalin from foxglove <u>will regulate</u> a person's heartbeat. _____

15. Australian Aborigines <u>use</u> kino from the bloodwood tree. _____

16. They say kino <u>will help</u> heal wounds, sores, and rashes. _____

Name

The **present perfect tense** of a verb tells about an action that has happened in the past and is still happening. It can also tell about something that happened at an indefinite time in the past. It is formed by combining *has* or *have* with the main verb called a **past participle**. Examples: Karen and I <u>have requested</u> books about octopuses from the library. The subject <u>has interested</u> us for some time.

Observing Octopuses

Write the present perfect tense of the verb in parentheses in each sentence.

1. I _____ that there are about 100 species of octopuses. (learn)

2. The mollusk _____ the respect of scientists. (earn)

3. Scientists _____ its ability to learn. (study)

4. Some octopuses _____ tasks learned by observation. (perform)

5. Octopuses _____ their own dens if no dens are available. (construct)

The **present progressive tense** of a verb tells about an action that is continuing now. Use present tense forms of **be**—*am, is, are*—with the **-ing** form of the main verb called the **present participle** to form the present progressive tense. Example: Karen and I <u>are looking</u> at octopuses in an aquarium.

The **past progressive tense** of a verb tells about an action that was continuing earlier. Use past tense forms of **be**—*was, were*—with the present participle to form the past progressive tense. Example: Karen and I <u>were visiting</u> with the marine biologist.

Write each sentence twice. Write the first with the present progressive tense of the verb in parentheses. Write the second with the past progressive tense.

Karen and I _____ an octopus in a tank. (watch)

6. _____

7. _____

The octopus's colors _____ right before our eyes. (change)

8. _____

9. _____

The frightened octopus _____ white! (turn)

10. _____

11. _____

Name _____

The **present perfect tense** of a verb tells about an action that has happened in the past and is still happening. It can also tell about something that happened at an indefinite time in the past. It is formed by combining *has* or *have* with the main verb called a **past participle**. Examples: A careless camper <u>has dropped</u> a match. Lighting <u>has struck</u> a tree.

Firestorm!

Write the present perfect tense of the verb in parentheses in each sentence.

1. Lightning _____ a fire in Yellowstone National Park. (start)

2. Old spruce and fir trees _____ quickly. (burn)

3. Flaming twigs _____ dry leaves on the forest floor. (ignite)

4. The winds _____ up, and the fire intensifies. (pick)

5. The wildfire _____ up the valley rapidly. (move)

The **present progressive tense** of a verb tells about an action that is continuing now. Use forms of **be**—*am, is, are*—with the **-ing** form of the main verb called the **present participle** to form the present progressive tense. Example: The flames <u>are growing</u> in intensity.

The **past progressive tense** of a verb tells about an action that was continuing earlier. Use past tense forms of **be**—*was, were*—and the past tense of **be**—*was, were*—with the present participle. Example: The winds <u>were beginning</u> to change direction.

Write each sentence twice. Write the first with the present progressive tense of the verb in parentheses. Write the second with the past progressive tense.

The fire _____ the dead leaves and debris on the ground. (consume)

6. _____

7. _____

The flames _____ into the forest canopy. (leap)

8. _____

9. _____

The flames _____ 200 feet into the air! (shoot)

10. _____

11. _____

Name _____

A **past tense verb** tells about something that has already happened. Most past tense verbs are formed by adding **–ed** to the present tense verb.

Irregular verbs have their own unique **past tense forms**.
Example: The mountain climbers <u>felt</u> confident. (feel)

The **present perfect tense** tells about something that has happened in the past and is still happening now. It can also tell about something that happened at an indefinite time in the past. Most present perfect tense verbs are formed by using *has* or *have* with the main verb called the past participle.

Irregular verbs have their own unique **present perfect tense forms**.
Example: The two climbers <u>have felt</u> they were capable of reaching the summit. (feel)

Mighty Matterhorn

Fill in the chart with the correct forms of the irregular verbs. Refer to a dictionary if needed.

Present	Past	Future
1. draw	_____	has or have _____
2. _____	swam	have or has _____
3. _____	_____	has or have taught

Complete each sentence with the past tense of the irregular verb in parentheses.

4. Two men _____ at the foot of a high peak in the Pennine Alps. (stand)

5. Heavy snow _____, and the storm raged around them. (fall)

6. They _____ only snow, ice, and the mountain. (see)

7. The Matterhorn _____ 14,692 feet above the valley. (rise)

8. Clouds _____ the summit from their view. (hide)

Complete each sentence with the present perfect tense of the irregular verb in parentheses.

9. They _____ of nothing else except the climb for months. (think)

10. The men _____ it would be difficult at this time of year. (know)

11. They _____ to make a direct assault on the Matterhorn. (choose)

12. The two climbers _____ their ascent. (begin)

13. Will they be the first ones to _____ it to the top? (make)

Name _____

Contractions

A **contraction** is made by joining two words to make one new word. One or more letters are left out. An **apostrophe** (') is used in place of the letter or letters left out. Contractions are very common in everyday speech and writing. Many contractions are made from a verb and the word *not*.
Example: do not/<u>don't</u> (An apostrophe takes the place of the *o* in *not*.)
Unusual spellings: cannot/<u>can't</u>, will not/<u>won't</u>

Some contractions are made by joining a pronoun and a verb.
Examples: I will/<u>I'll</u>, who is/<u>who's</u>, he would/<u>he'd</u>, they are/<u>they're</u>

Some contractions are made by joining a noun and a verb.
Examples: The <u>disc's</u> flying through the air. (disc is) <u>Pat's</u> throwing the disc. (Pat is)

Flying Discs

Write the two words from which each contraction is made.

1. shouldn't _____   2. they'll _____

3. I'd _____   4. you're _____

5. what's _____   6. hadn't _____

7. couldn't _____   8. Sherri's _____

Write the contraction for each pair of words.

9. was not _____   10. they would _____

11. he will _____   12. that is _____

13. you have _____   14. they have _____

15. where is _____

16. he is _____

Rewrite the sentences on another sheet of paper substituting contractions for the underlined words.

17. Flying discs <u>are not</u> all the same size, shape, or color.

18. Pat <u>cannot</u> decide which of hers to use today.

19. <u>She is</u> planning to meet her friends at the park.

20. <u>They are</u> going to practice some throws.

21. Pat <u>does not</u> do a floater well, so <u>that is</u> the throw <u>she will</u> practice.

Name

Read or listen to the directions. Fill in the circle beside the best answer.

☐ Example:

Which word is not a present tense action verb?

(A) fasten   (B) knead

(C) appear   (D) glide

Answer: C because it does not show action.

Always read each question carefully.

Now try these. You have 20 minutes. Continue until you see (STOP).

Which sentences in 1 and 2 do not have action verbs?

1. (A) Shallow seas are interesting diving sites.

   (B) Marine biologists dive to study plants and animals.

   (C) They wear a cylinder of compressed air on their backs.

   (D) They take photographs to study later.

2. (A) Marine archaeologists search for sunken ships.

   (B) They study artifacts found in wrecks.

   (C) They learn about the ship's cargo and about how the crew lived.

   (D) Finding sunken ships is not easy, however.

---

3. Which sentence has a present tense action verb?

   (A) There are three main kinds of hyenas.

   (B) Spotted hyenas are the most common.

   (C) Hyenas hunt antelope and zebras.

   (D) They are predators.

GO ON

4. Which sentence has a present tense linking verb?

    (A) Hyenas are scavengers.

    (B) They often scavenge from lions' kills.

    (C) They eat almost any part of an animal.

    (D) They warn other hyenas of danger.

5. Which sentence does not have a past tense action verb?

    (A) Eric entered the cave cautiously.

    (B) The beam of his flashlight casts eerie shadows.

    (C) Stalagmites grew up from the cave floor.

    (D) He heard a waterfall in the distance.

6. Which sentence has a past tense linking verb?

    (A) Hundreds of stalactites were overhead.

    (B) A small underground lake glistened in the pale light.

    (C) Eric walked farther into the cave.

    (D) He explored the cave for hours.

Which are the correct past tenses of the action verbs in 7 and 8?

7. carry	carryed (A)	carried (B)	carries (C)	caryd (D)
8. prepare	prepared (A)	preparred (B)	preparied (C)	prepares (D)

GO ON ▷

9. Which sentence has a future tense verb?

    (A) Tanya enjoys reading tall tales.

    (B) Her favorite story is about Pecos Bill.

    (C) She reads the story often.

    (D) She will tell you the story if you ask her.

Which sentences in 10 and 11 have present perfect tense verbs?

10. (A) Carlos has wanted to visit the zoo for some time.

    (B) He knows there is a new baby elephant on display.

    (C) The baby's name is Raja.

    (D) Carlos will ask his best friend, Roy, to go with him.

11. (A) The boys have enjoyed their friendship for several years.

    (B) They first met at soccer practice in third grade.

    (C) Carlos and Ray are teammates again this year.

    (D) They also play baseball together.

12. What is the present progressive tense of **rotate**?

rotates	is rotating	was rotating	have rotated
(A)	(B)	(C)	(D)

Which sentences in 13 and 14 have present progressive tense verbs?

13. (A) Andrew is learning about armadillos at school.

    (B) He lives in Texas where there are many armadillos.

    (C) There have been armadillos in Texas for many years.

    (D) Armadillos in Texas have nine narrow bands of armor.

GO ON

Unit 2 Test

14. (A) An armadillo is a strange-looking creature.

    (B) Its body is covered with a bony shell called a carapace.

    (C) It uses its shell for protection.

    (D) Some scientists are calling armadillos mini-dinosaurs.

Which sentences in 15 and 16 have past progressive tense verbs?

15. (A) Andrew's class was watching a video about armadillos.

    (B) The armadillo's diet seemed strange to Andrew.

    (C) Maggots and fire ants were on the armadillo's menu!

    (D) Armadillos also eat roots, dirt, and debris.

16. (A) Armadillos cannot see or hear well.

    (B) However, armadillos have an amazing sense of smell.

    (C) They were probing in the ground for insects they could smell.

    (D) They do not have to travel far to find food.

---

17. What is the past tense of the irregular verb **bring**?

brought	has brought	brings	NG
(A)	(B)	(C)	(D)

---

18. What is the present perfect tense of the irregular verb **fly**?

have flown	flies	flew	flying
(A)	(B)	(C)	(D)

---

19. What is the present perfect tense of the irregular verb **find**?

finds	found	was finding	NG
(A)	(B)	(C)	(D)

GO ON

20. Which sentence does not have a contraction?

(A) Dave's mother had an operation.

(B) She won't be able to drive for six weeks.

(C) Who's going to take him to karate lesson?

(D) He doesn't want to miss a class.

Choose which verb tense you should use if you want to tell about an action that has happened in the past and is continuing to happen: present, past, present perfect, present progressive, or past progressive. Write a sentence containing the verb tense you chose.

_____

_____

_____

_____

Name

Adjectives

An **adjective** is a word that describes a noun. It can tell how many or what kind. An adjective often comes in front of the noun it describes. Example: The <u>red</u> kayak bobbed up and down in the river.

An adjective can come after a linking verb. A linking verb connects the subject part of a sentence with an adjective in the predicate. Example: The river was <u>white</u> with foam.

A sentence may have more than one adjective. Example: <u>Foaming</u>, <u>swirling</u> waters were ahead of us.

White Water Ahead!

Write the adjective or adjectives that describe each noun in bold type.

1. White-water kayaking is a thrilling **adventure**. _____

2. A kayak is a boat with a closed top and a watertight **cockpit**. _____

3. The small boat is guided by a person using a two-bladed **paddle**. _____

4. Wearing a protective **helmet** is mandatory. _____

5. A paddler should always wear a life **vest**. _____

6. A wet suit is important to wear in icy, mountain **streams**. _____, _____

7. What is it like to challenge a raging **river** or stream? _____

8. It takes strength and skill to guide a kayak through jagged **rocks**. _____

9. There may be swift, treacherous **currents**. _____, _____

10. Kayak with experienced **paddlers**—never alone. _____

Underline the adjective and circle the noun it describes in each sentence.

11. Fiberglass kayaks can take a beating.

12. They usually return to their original shape.

13. Wooden boats would be wrecked on the rocks.

Underline adjectives that could complete this sentence: Kayaking can be ___ .

14. dangerous	15. unsafe	16. thrilling	17. very
18. boating	19. exciting	20. perilous	21. risky
22. scary	23. difficult	24. popular	25. fun

Adjectives: comparative and superlative   Unit 3

An **adjective** is used to compare persons, places, and things. Add **-er** to most adjectives when comparing two nouns. Add **-est** to most adjectives when comparing more than two nouns. Example: clear/clear<u>er</u>/clear<u>est</u>

If the adjective ends in silent **-e**, drop the **-e** before adding **-er** or **-est**. Example: blue/blu<u>er</u>/blu<u>est</u>

If a one-syllable adjective has a consonant-vowel-consonant pattern, double the final consonant before adding **-er** or **-est**. Example: flat/flat<u>ter</u>/flat<u>test</u>

If an adjective ends in **-y**, change the **-y** to **-i** and add **-er** or **-est**. Example: funny/funn<u>ier</u>/funn<u>iest</u>

Use **more** before most adjectives that have more than two syllables to compare two nouns. Use **most** before most adjectives that have more than two syllables to compare more than two nouns. Example: colorful/<u>more</u> colorful/<u>most</u> colorful

Use **more** and **most** with some two-syllable adjectives that do not use **-er** endings. Example: awful/<u>more</u> awful/<u>most</u> awful

Promises, Promises

Follow the rules above to complete the chart with adjectives that can compare nouns.

Adjectives	Adjectives That Compare Two Nouns	Adjectives That Compare More Than Two Nouns
1. skinny	_____	_____
2. light	_____	_____
3. terrible	_____	_____
4. exceptional	_____	_____
5. flimsy	_____	_____
6. white	_____	_____
7. desirable	_____	_____
8. thin	_____	_____

Underline the correct adjective in parentheses to complete each sentence.

9. My sister is (responsible, more responsible) than I am for this messy room.

10. Mother says it is the (messier, messiest) room she has ever seen.

11. We promised we would be (most trustworthy, more trustworthy) in the future.

Name

Predicate adjectives, proper adjectives, and proper nouns

A **predicate adjective** is an adjective used after a linking verb to describe the subject of the sentence. Example: The legend is old. (Old is an adjective that describes *legend*. *Is* is the linking verb.)

A **proper noun** names a special person, place, or thing. Some proper nouns are used as adjectives. A proper noun begins with a capital letter. Example: The Native American legend is old. (The proper noun Native American is used to describe *legend*.)

A **proper adjective** can sometimes be formed by adding an ending to a proper noun. It begins with a capital letter. Example: The American West has many legends. (American is made by adding an ending to the proper noun *America*. American describes the *West*.)

Big Bend National Park

Read each sentence. Write **1** if the word in bold type is a predicate adjective, **2** if the word is a proper adjective, or **3** if the word is a proper noun.

_____ 1. Big Bend National Park in Texas is **remote**.

_____ 2. The park is named after a big turn in the **Rio Grande River**.

_____ 3. An old legend said the **Great Spirit** created the park's canyons and mountains.

_____ 4. **Comanche** raiders used to hide in the mountains years ago.

_____ 5. The United States Calvary patrolled the border with **Mexico**.

_____ 6. They were looking for **Mexican** bandits.

_____ 7. Roadrunners and rattlesnakes live in the **Chihuahaun** Desert.

_____ 8. The Lucifer hummingbird is **one** of 450 species of birds in the park.

_____ 9. Big Bend National Park is the only nesting site of the **Colima** warbler.

_____ 10. **Emory Peak** is the highest peak in the park.

Write a sentence with a proper adjective. Tell from which proper noun it is formed.

Name

Articles

A, **an**, and **the** are special adjectives called **articles**. Use **a** to describe any singular noun that begins with a consonant sound. Use **an** to describe any singular noun that begins with a vowel sound. Use **the** with singular or plural nouns to tell about a particular person, place, or thing. Examples: <u>a</u> teacher/<u>the</u> teacher, <u>an</u> analyst/<u>the</u> analyst, <u>the</u> typists

Career Paths

Write **a** or **an** in front of each singular noun. Write **the** in front of each plural noun.

1. _____ employee
2. _____ duchess
3. _____ professional
4. _____ actress
5. _____ monarchs
6. _____ candidates
7. _____ designer
8. _____ official
9. _____ architect
10. _____ rangers
11. _____ troopers
12. _____ musicians
13. _____ forester
14. _____ ventriloquist
15. _____ gymnast
16. _____ instructors

Sometimes the noun is preceded by one or more adjectives. Use **a** in front of an adjective that begins with a consonant sound. Example: <u>a</u> talented author (The article no longer precedes the noun beginning with a vowel, so use <u>a</u>, not *an*.)

Use **an** in front of an adjective that begins with a vowel sound. Example: <u>an</u> amazing musician (The article no longer precedes the noun beginning with a consonant sound, so use <u>an</u>, not *a*.)

Use the articles **a** and **an** correctly with the phrases below.

17. _____ cave explorer
18. _____ old cobbler
19. _____ nuclear engineer
20. _____ angry salesperson
21. _____ avid fisherman
22. _____ professional artist
23. _____ radio announcer
24. _____ remarkable ecologist
25. _____ outstanding poet
26. _____ brave astronaut

Name

Adverbs   Unit 3

An **adverb** is a word that tells how, when, or where the action of the verb takes place.
Adverbs that tell how often end in **–ly**.
Examples: The prospector <u>slowly</u> bent <u>down</u> on the riverbank <u>today</u>.
                    (how)   (where)   (when)

All the Glitters

Write the adverb or adverbs that describe the action of the verb in bold type.

1. The prospector **looked** down into the pan. _____

2. He **found** a gold nugget there. _____

3. The old man **studied** the nugget carefully. _____

4. Other prospectors **lined** the riverbank nearby. _____

5. The man **turned** around to see if anyone was watching. _____

6. Then the prospector **put** the nugget deep into his pocket. _____, _____

7. His heart **beat** rapidly with the excitement of finding gold. _____

8. The old prospector **dipped** his pan into the river again. _____

9. He eagerly **scooped** up the rock, sand, and gravel. _____, _____

10. The man gently **sifted** the contents of the pan. _____

11. Disappointed at finding nothing, he **put** away his prospecting tools. _____

12. He **would return** tomorrow and renew his search for gold. _____

Write each adverb from above under the correct heading.

Adverbs That Tell How   **Adverbs That Tell When**   **Adverbs That Tell Where**

_____   _____   _____

_____   _____   _____

_____   _____   _____

_____   _____

                                                                _____

                                                                _____

                                                                _____

Name

Adverbs: comparative and superlative

An **adverb** is a word that tells how, when, or where the action of the verb takes place.
Add **–er** to one-syllable adverbs to compare two actions. Add **–est** to one-syllable
adverbs to compare more than two actions. Examples: quick/quick<u>er</u>/quick<u>est</u>
Unusual spellings: far/farth<u>er</u>/farth<u>est</u>

Adverbs often end in **–ly**. Use **more** preceding these adverbs to compare two actions.
Use **most** when comparing more than two actions.
Examples: carefully/<u>more</u> carefully/<u>most</u> carefully

Political Ambitions

Complete the chart with adverbs that compare the actions of verbs.

Adverbs	Adverbs That Compare Two Verbs	Adverbs That Compare More Than Two Verbs
1. completely	_____	_____
2. fondly	_____	_____
3. near	_____	_____
4. wearily	_____	_____
5. close	_____	_____
6. brilliantly	_____	_____
7. timely	_____	_____
8. seriously	_____	_____

Complete each sentence with the correct adverb in parentheses.

9. Clark ran his campaign for Student Council president _____ than Tina. (more successfully, most successfully)

10. He made speeches _____ than his opponents. (often, more often)

11. Clark spoke _____ about his plans for the student government. (truthfully, most truthfully)

12. Students _____ voted for Clark after hearing his ideas. (gladly, most gladly)

13. He beat Tina and his other opponents _____. (handily, more handily)

Negatives

A **negative** is a word used to make a sentence mean "no." *No, no one, not, nothing, never, nobody, nowhere,* and contractions formed from a verb and *not* are negative words.

Only use one negative word in a sentence.

Example: I <u>never</u> knew there were 70,000 species of fungi.

A **double negative** is the incorrect use of two negative words in a sentence.

Example: I <u>never</u> knew <u>nothing</u> about fungi.

The sentence can be corrected by either removing *never* or by replacing *nothing* with *anything*. I knew <u>nothing</u> about fungi. I <u>never</u> knew *anything* about fungi.

Fungi Facts

Study the chart showing words that can replace a second negative in a sentence.

Negative	Positive	Negative	Positive
no	a, any, one	nobody	anybody, somebody
no one	anyone, someone	nowhere	anywhere, somewhere
nothing	anything, something	never	ever

Underline the two negative words in each sentence. Rewrite each sentence. Correct it by replacing the second negative with a word from the chart.

1. A mushroom isn't no plant.

    _____

2. They never had no roots, stems, or leaves like plants.

    _____

3. No one never told me that fungi feed on living dead plants and animals.

    _____

4. Nowhere did I read nothing saying that fungi can digest almost everything.

    _____

5. Mushrooms are fungi, but poisonous ones are never no good to eat.

    _____

6. Haven't you never had mold grow on old bread or fruit?

    _____

7. You wouldn't want to eat no food with mold on it.

    _____

Prepositions and prepositional phrases   Unit 3

A **preposition** is a word that describes a relationship between words in a sentence. Example: The steamboat <u>on</u> *the Mississippi River* carried cotton. (The preposition <u>on</u> introduces the phrase *the Mississippi River*. This **prepositional phrase** tells the relationship of the steamboat and the Mississippi River.)

A preposition must have an object. Example: The steamboat captain looked <u>down</u> the *gangplank*. (*Gangplank* is the object of the preposition.) In the sentence "The steamboat captain looked down," *down* has no object. It is an adverb. Prepositional phrases can act like adverbs in a sentence by telling where or when.

On the Rivers of America

There are about 60 prepositions. Some of the most common are **at, by, in, for, on, to,** and **with**. Underline the prepositions and circle the objects of the prepositions in these prepositional phrases.

1. in the 1850's
2. above the trees
3. up the river
4. between two rows
5. by the sandbars
6. on the route
7. around the bend
8. for an entire day
9. at the controls
10. under the branch

Underline the prepositions and circle the objects of the prepositions in the sentences.

11. Robert Fulton built the first commercially successful steamboat in 1807.

12. The *Clermont* carried passengers on the Hudson River in New York.

13. In 1811, Fulton's steamboat *New Orleans* began a trip from Louisville, Kentucky.

14. The steamboat's destination was the city of New Orleans.

15. The captain had to steer the boat through rapids on the Ohio River.

16. Then a strong earthquake hit a large area of the Mississippi River.

17. It changed the river so much that the captain was unsure of his surroundings.

18. Next, hostile Native Americans followed the *New Orleans* in their war canoes.

19. Finally, the steamboat reached New Orleans at the southern end of the Mississippi.

20. Fulton proved that it was possible for a steamboat to carry passengers and cargo through the Mississippi and its tributaries.

Prepositions and prepositional phrases

A **preposition** is a word that describes a relationship between words in a sentence. Example: Land iguanas live <u>in</u> *dry places*. (The preposition <u>in</u> introduces the phrase *dry places*. This **prepositional phrase** tells the relationship of the iguana and dry places to iguanas. Prepositional phrases can act like adverbs in sentences. *In dry places* tells where the iguanas live.)

A preposition must have an object.

Example: Marine iguanas feed <u>on</u> *seaweed*. (*Seaweed* is the object of the preposition.)

Some words can be either prepositions or adverbs. A preposition must have an object. If there is no object, the word is probably an adverb.

Example: The tortoise lived <u>inside</u> the *crater*. The tortoise moved <u>inside</u>.
             (preposition) (object)   (adverb)

The Amazing Galápagos Islands

Underline the prepositions and circle the objects of the prepositions in the sentences.

1. The Galápagos Islands are 600 miles off the coast of Ecuador, South America.

2. These volcanic islands in the Pacific Ocean were completely barren after they formed.

3. Only birds that nested on rocks lived on the islands at first.

4. Then tiny, light seeds were carried to the islands on the trade winds.

5. The beginnings of plant life made it possible for other animals to inhabit the islands.

6. Ocean currents carried seeds that washed up on the shores and took root.

7. The winds also carried bees, butterflies, and other tiny creatures from the mainland.

8. Now the Galápagos Islands are home to the world's only marine iguanas.

9. Giant tortoises are found in the craters of old volcanoes.

10. The Galápagos hawk is a predator that also scavenges on the bodies of dead animals.

11. Vampire finches feed on the blood of other birds.

12. American oystercatchers lay their eggs among the rocks on these volcanic islands.

13. Albatrosses make round-trip flights from the islands to the coast of South America.

14. The Ecuadoran government made the Galápagos Islands a national park in 1959.

15. People cannot build new homes on the islands.

16. Environmentalists hope to save the fragile ecology of the islands.

43

Name _____

Interjections   Unit 3

An **interjection** is a word or words that often expresses strong emotion that might relate to surprise, pain, sorrow, anger, or relief. Use an exclamation mark after an interjection that stands alone.

Interjections that can stand alone: *Aha! Golly! Good grief! Great! Hey! My! My goodness! My, oh, my! Oh! Oh boy! Oh my! Oh no! Oh oh! Oops! Ouch! Ow! Phew! Wow!*
Example: <u>Ow!</u> I think I've been stung.

An interjection may be part of a sentence when it expresses mild emotion. Use a comma to separate the interjection from the sentence. Example: <u>Oh my</u>, that looks like a bee sting.

Interjections such as *well, why,* and *oh* are used as fillers. Use a comma to separate the interjection from the sentence. Examples: <u>Well</u>, I believe you're right. <u>Why</u>, I believe you're right. <u>Oh</u>, I believe you're right.

Interjections such as *hey there* and *say* are attention-getters.
Examples: <u>Hey there</u>, come here. <u>Say</u>, that looks painful.

Oh Oh! Stingers!

Underline the interjection in each sentence.

1. Oh my, there's a wasp nest in the tree by the garage.

2. Oh boy! I don't want to get stung by a wasp.

3. Say, did you know that as many as 2,000 wasps may live in a nest?

4. Two thousand wasps! Good grief!

5. Well, wasps aren't all bad, because they eat many insects that are pests.

6. Oh, I didn't know that, but I still don't want to get stung.

7. Hey! I think the wasps are heading this way.

8. Phew! That was close.

Complete each sentence with a different interjection. Determine if the sentence needs a strong or mild interjection, a filler, or an attention-getter. Use the correct punctuation.

9. _____ there are many interesting facts about bees and hornets in this book.

10. It says bumblebees' wings beat 200 times per second! _____

11. _____ a honeybee dies after it stings someone.

12. I've been stung before, and it hurt a lot. _____

13. _____ it's a good thing you weren't stung by a hornet.

14. Hornets are the largest stinging insects in the world. _____

Coordinating conjunctions

And and **but** are the most common **coordinating conjunctions** used to connect words, phrases, clauses, and sentences.

And is used to connect two words, two subjects, or two predicates with like ideas. Examples: The first *sea turtles* <u>and</u> *dinosaurs* lived 200 millions years ago. (<u>And</u> connects two subjects.) Sea turtles became *smaller* <u>and</u> *smaller* as they evolved. (<u>And</u> connects two words that are adjectives.) Sea turtles *are cold-blooded* <u>and</u> *have scaly skin.* (<u>And</u> connects two predicates.)

And is used to connect two sentences with like ideas to form a compound sentence. Example: Sea turtles are cold-blooded. They have scaly skin. *Sea turtles are cold-blooded,* <u>and</u> *they have scaly skin.*

But connects words, phrases, clauses, and sentences with differing ideas. Example: *Sea turtles are found in warm ocean waters,* <u>but</u> *they are not found in cold waters.*

Sensational Sea Turtles

Identify the coordinating conjunctions as connecting **words**, **subjects**, **predicates**, or **sentences**. Write the answers on the lines.

1. Sea turtles evolved over millions of years, and they are among the oldest surviving creatures on Earth. _____

2. A sea turtle's top shell is called a carapace, and its bottom shell is called a plastron. _____

3. A sea turtle can swim 20 miles an hour, but a human swims less than five miles an hour. _____

4. A turtle's strong front and back flippers make it a powerful swimmer. _____

5. Sea turtles have good hearing and eyesight. _____

6. Sea turtles cannot pull their heads, feet, and tails inside their shells. _____

7. Kemp's ridley turtles and olive ridley turtles are the smallest sea turtles. _____

8. Even so, they can weigh 100 pounds and measure two feet in length. _____

Name

Unit 3 Test
Page 1

Grammar: Parts of Speech—Adjectives, Articles, Adverbs, Negatives, Prepositions, Interjections, and Conjunctions

Read or listen to the directions. Fill in the circle beside the best answer.

☐ Example:

Which word is an adjective in this sentence?

The air we breathe is thickest at Earth's surface.

(A) air   (B) breathe

(C) thickest   (D) surface

Answer: C because it describes the air we breathe.

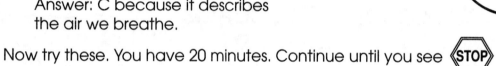

Now try these. You have 20 minutes. Continue until you see STOP .

Which words are adjectives in sentences 1 and 2?

1. A northerly wind comes from the north and blows toward the south.

2. Commonwealth Bay in Antarctica is the windiest place on Earth.

Antarctica (A)   windiest (B)   place (C)   Earth (D)

3. Which line of poetry from "The Eagle" by Lord Alfred Tennyson does not have an adjective?

(A) "The wrinkled sea beneath him crawls;"

(B) "He watches from his mountain walls,"

(C) "And like a thunderbolt he falls."

(D) NG

GO ON ➡

Fill in the answer circles completely and neatly.

© Carson-Dellosa CD-4314   **46**   Teach & Test Language: Grade 5

Choose an adjective that describes each noun in 4 and 5.

4. principal

(A) reliable   (B) eagerness   (C) sincerity   (D) study

5. journal

(A) ambition   (B) bravery   (C) legible   (D) learned

Choose the correct form of the adjectives to complete sentences 6 and 7.

6. The advertisement was the _____ one in the newspaper.

(A) effective   (B) most effective   (C) more effective

7. The book is _____ than the last book we read.

(A) interesting   (B) more interesting   (C) most interesting

8. In which phrase is the article used incorrectly?

(A) a ugly baboon   (B) a huge elephant

(C) an imaginary unicorn   (D) an active monkey

9. Which sentence contains a proper adjective?

(A) Have you ever been to China?

(B) China has the world's largest population.

(C) The Chinese have many ancient customs.

(D) The Chinese people are very friendly.

GO ON

Unit 3 Test

10. Which sentence contains a predicate adjective?

(A) Koalas look adorable.

(B) Koalas eat eucalyptus leaves.

(C) Koalas live in Australia.

(D) Wild koalas rarely drink water.

Which words are adverbs in sentences 11 and 12?

11. Someday my family and I may visit Australia.

Someday	may	visit	Australia
(A)	(B)	(C)	(D)

12. I think I will start reading about Australia now.

think	start	reading	NG
(A)	(B)	(C)	(D)

13. Which sentence does not contain an adverb?

(A) The weather suddenly became colder.

(B) The wind blew fiercely.

(C) The snow fell on the mountain.

(D) We drove cautiously on the road.

14. Which form of the adverb completes the sentence correctly?

The firefighter _____ walked into the burning building.

more courageously	courageously	most courageously
(A)	(B)	(C)

GO ON ⟶

15. Which sentence is correctly written?

(A) There is no river longer than the Nile River.

(B) I never knew no river was longer than the Amazon.

(C) Kathy can't never believe there are rivers longer than the Missouri River.

(D) Didn't nobody check the atlas to see which is true?

16. Which sentence does not contain a prepositional phrase?

(A) Grizzly bears are large and potentially dangerous animals.

(B) Some grizzlies live along the coast of Alaska.

(C) Their fur can vary from light brown to black.

(D) They feed primarily on plants.

17. Which word is the object of the preposition?

Grizzly bears have long claws on their front paws.

bears
(A)

claws
(B)

their
(C)

paws
(D)

18. Which sentence does not contain an interjection?

(A) Mammoth Cave in Kentucky has almost 360 miles of tunnels.

(B) Wow, no wonder they call it Mammoth.

(C) Well, it is the world's largest known cave system.

(D) Say, I would like to visit it.

GO ON

19. What does the conjunction **and** connect in the sentence?

Fountains of steam and boiling water are called geysers.

subjects	predicates	sentences	words
(A)	(B)	(C)	(D)

20. Which sentence does not use the correct conjunction?

(A) The Alps and the Himalayas are mountain ranges.

(B) The Alps are in Europe, and the Himalayas are in Asia.

(C) The Alps are only a few million years old, the Himalayas are over 50 million years old.

(D) Mount Everest and Mount Blanc are high mountain peaks.

Write a sentence using **down** as an adverb. Write another using **down** as a preposition. Explain how this word can be used as two different parts of speech.

_____

_____

_____

_____

_____

_____

STOP

Name

Four kinds of sentences   Unit 4

There are four kinds of sentences: **declarative**, **interrogative**, **exclamatory**, and **imperative**.

A **declarative sentence**, also called a statement, tells a complete thought. It ends with a period (**.**). Example: Hector is on the track team.

An **interrogative sentence**, also called a question, asks something. It ends with a question mark (**?**). Example: What event does Hector run?

An **exclamatory sentence** shows great emotion. It ends with an exclamation mark (**!**). An exclamatory sentence often begins or ends with an interjection such as *wow*. The interjection is separated from the rest of the sentence by a comma. Example: Wow, a mile!

An **imperative sentence**, also called a **command**, gives an order. It ends with a period (**.**). Example: Take me to the next track meet.

Mighty Mountains

Identify each of the following sentences. Write **D** for a declarative sentence, **INT** for an interrogative sentence, **E** for an exclamatory sentence, or **IMP** for an imperative sentence on the line. Add the correct ending mark.

_____ 1. Mountains rise where Earth's surface is under pressure

_____ 2. Is Earth still forming mountains

_____ 3. Yes, and some of the old ones are wearing away

_____ 4. Tell me how that happens

_____ 5. Does the wind and rain wear them down

_____ 6. Yes, but it takes millions of years for that to happen

_____ 7. Is that why the Appalachians are more rounded than the Rocky Mountains

_____ 8. Right, the Appalachians are about 150 million years older than the Rockies

_____ 9. Wow, that makes them 250 million years old

_____ 10. What is the highest mountain in the United States

_____ 11. Golly, Mt. McKinley is 20,320 feet tall

_____ 12. That also makes it the tallest mountain in North America

 On another sheet of paper, write one example of each type of sentence: declarative, interrogative, exclamatory, and imperative.

Declarative and imperative sentences   Unit 4

A **declarative sentence**, also called a statement, tells a complete thought.
It ends with a period (**.**). Example: I would like to try windsurfing.

An **imperative sentence**, also called a command, gives an order. There is no written or spoken subject in an imperative sentence. However, *you*, both singular and plural, is the implied subject. The sentence ends with a period (**.**). Example: (You) Let me help you.

Windsurfing

Identify each sentence as either a declarative sentence or an imperative sentence. Write **D** for declarative or **I** for imperative.

_____ 1. Windsurfing is a popular outdoor activity.

_____ 2. Tell me about windsurfing.

_____ 3. Windsurfers ride a board with a sail on water.

_____ 4. Give me tips for learning how to windsurf.

_____ 5. Boards with flat bottoms are best for beginners.

_____ 6. The rig consists of the sail, the boom, and the mast.

_____ 7. The rig is connected to the board by the universal joint.

_____ 8. Stand on the board and raise the rig with the uphaul rope.

_____ 9. You need good balance to do this because a wet sail is heavy.

_____ 10. Hold onto the boom.

_____ 11. The boom is used for steering, changing speed, and keeping your balance.

_____ 12. Practice with an experienced windsurfer before going out on your own.

_____ 13. Wear a life jacket when windsurfing.

Pretend you are going to teach a friend how to do something for the first time. Write four imperative sentences giving the person directions. Try to use a different verb in each sentence.

1. _____

2. _____

3. _____

4. _____

Name

Interrogative and exclamatory sentences

An **interrogative sentence** asks a question. It ends with a question mark (**?**).
Example: What are carnivorous plants?

An **exclamatory sentence** shows great emotion. It ends with an exclamation mark (**!**).
An exclamatory sentence often begins or ends with an interjection, such as *wow*.
The interjection is separated from the rest of the sentence by a comma.
Example: Good grief, they're plants that eat animals!

Carnivorous Plants!

Identify each sentence as either an interrogative sentence–**I** or
an exclamatory sentence–**E**. Add the correct ending mark.

_____ 1. How many kinds of carnivorous plants are there

_____ 2. Wow, four hundred fifty species

_____ 3. What are some examples of what the plants eat

_____ 4. Oh no, spiders, insects, frogs and mice

_____ 5. Where do these meat-eating plants live

_____ 6. Do they live in swamps and marshes

_____ 7. What are the ways they lure animals to them

_____ 8. Goodness, some carnivorous plants smell like nectar to bees

_____ 9. Phew, some smell like rot and decay

_____ 10. Do some plants have sticky leaves that trap insects

_____ 11. Does the Venus flytrap have leaves that open and then shut around its prey

_____ 12. Ugh, then the Venus flytrap drowns its victim in digestive juices

Write 10 words that are often used
to begin questions.

_____ _____

_____ _____

_____ _____

_____ _____

_____ _____

Write four
interrogative sentences
about carnivorous plants.
Begin each question with
a different word from
your list.

Sentences, fragments, and run-ons

Unit 4

A **declarative sentence** tells a complete thought.
Example: Native Americans lived in North America long before Europeans arrived.

A **fragment** does not. Example: In the 1500's.

A **run-on sentence** has too many thoughts, often strung together with commas. The thoughts are not connected correctly with a conjunction or with the correct punctuation. Example: Early Native American cultures adapted to the regions in which they lived, some lived in coastal regions.

Early Americans

Write **D** for declarative sentence, **F** for fragment, or **R** for run-on.

_____ 1. Native American people who lived on the coasts hunted sea creatures.

_____ 2. And gathered shellfish.

_____ 3. Those who lived on inland rivers and lakes speared and netted fish.

_____ 4. The Plains Indians followed the buffalo herds, they hunted them and killed them by throwing spears or shooting arrows or running them over cliffs to their deaths.

_____ 5. Forest-dwellers hunted deer and small animals.

_____ 6. Their houses varied.

_____ 7. Some Native Americans lived in farming communities, they grew corn and beans and squash in small plots or large fields.

_____ 8. The Pueblo Indians lived in the desert Southwest.

_____ 9. They farmed and hunted deer, elk, and rabbit.

_____ 10. Life changed for the Pueblo people when the Spanish explorers arrived.

_____ 11. And claimed the land for Spain in the 1500's.

_____ 12. The Spanish army officers forced the Pueblo Indians to work for them building roads and buildings and working in mines and on farms, Christian missionaries outlawed their religion.

Rewrite one of the run-on sentences to make better declarative sentences.

_____

_____

_____

Name

Simple subjects and predicates

A declarative sentence has a subject that tells who or what the statement is about. It has a noun or pronoun that is called the **simple subject**. Example: <u>Many people</u> immigrated to America in the 1900's. (The complete subject is underlined. *People* is the simple subject.)

A declarative sentence has a predicate that tells what the subject does or is. It contains an action verb or a linking verb that is called the **simple predicate**. Example: Most of them <u>landed in New York Harbor</u>. (The complete predicate is underlined. *Landed* is the simple predicate.)

Where Dreams Come True

Circle the simple subject and underline the simple predicate in each sentence.

1. A little boy's father hoisted the child up on his shoulders.

2. They stood on the deck of a ship with hundreds of other people.

3. These European immigrants had traveled for weeks to reach America.

4. The passengers wanted to get a better look at something ahead.

5. It was the Statue of Liberty holding the torch of freedom.

6. The excited crowd cheered in many different languages.

7. Tears of happiness and joy ran down the cheeks of many persons.

8. The people saw a busy harbor with steamships, tugboats, and ferryboats.

9. The tall buildings of New York City rose in the distance.

10. The newcomers transferred from the ship to smaller crafts.

11. The river barges carried America's new arrivals to Ellis Island.

12. Ellis Island was a United States reception center for immigrants.

13. Over 12 million people passed through Ellis Island in 60 years.

14. The busiest years were between 1918 and 1924.

15. Today, the National Park Service operates the Ellis Island Immigration Museum.

16. The museum's exhibits include recordings of immigrants sharing their memories of their arrival in America.

Read an article in the newspaper. Find the simple subject and simple predicate in each sentence.

Complete subjects and predicates

The subject of a sentence tells who or what the sentence is about. The **complete subject** contains a noun or pronoun, called the simple subject, and any words that complement it. Example: <u>Ocean tides</u> go in and out twice a day. (The complete subject is underlined. *Tides* is the simple subject.)

The predicate of a sentence tells what the subject does or is. The **complete predicate** contains an action verb or a linking verb, called the simple predicate, and any words that complement it. Example: The pull of gravity <u>causes the tides</u>. (The complete predicate is underlined. *Causes* is the simple predicate.)

Tide Pool Tale

Underline the complete subject with one line and circle the simple subject. Underline the complete predicate with two lines and circle the simple predicate.

1. A young girl walks carefully along the rocky shore.

2. Carmen notices the tide going out.

3. Pools of water collect in rocky crevices along the shore.

4. Tide pools are homes to sea plants and animals.

5. Seaweeds are the most common tide pool plants.

6. They provide food and shelter for a variety of animals.

7. Carmen watches a sea urchin attached to a rock.

8. Sea urchins are little spiny animals with tiny tube feet.

9. Their mouths are on their undersides.

10. Their sharp teeth cut seaweed into little pieces.

11. Carmen spies an abalone at another tide pool.

12. This mollusk clings to a rock as it munches kelp.

13. Carmen sees many barnacles attached to the tide pool rocks.

14. Barnacles close their shells during low tide.

15. These crustaceans wait for feeding time at high tide.

16. Carmen watches as the tide creeps back up the beach.

Name

Compound subjects and predicates

A **compound subject** has two or more simple subjects joined by *and*.
Example: <u>Mariculture</u> *and* <u>aquaculture</u> are the practices of growing plants and animals that live naturally in water. (The sentence has two simple subjects joined by *and*.)

A **compound predicate** has two or more simple predicates joined by *and*. The simple predicates have the same subject. Example: Mariculture <u>specifically refers to</u> *and* <u>limits the practice to</u> saltwater plants and animals.

Farming in the Sea

Read each sentence. Write **CS** if the sentence has a compound subject. Circle the two simple subjects. Write **CP** if it has a compound predicate. Circle the two simple predicates. Write **N** if the sentence has neither a compound subject nor a compound predicate.

_____ 1. People began planting crops and raising animals about 10,000 years ago.

_____ 2. The ancient Chinese and Japanese practiced freshwater and saltwater farming.

_____ 3. The Japanese raised oysters as early as 2000 B.C.

_____ 4. Fish and shellfish have long been sources of protein for Southeast Asian people.

_____ 5. Overfishing and pollution led to the decline of ocean animals over the years.

_____ 6. Sea farming and ranching help restore the food supply.

_____ 7. Mariculturists, or sea farmers, raise and sell lobsters and shrimp.

_____ 8. Oysters grown in farms often grow larger and taste better than wild oysters.

_____ 9. Tuna and salmon are in high demand.

_____ 10. Seaweeds are widely farmed in Southeast Asia for a variety of uses.

Write four declarative sentences about your friends, classmates, school, and the subjects you study. Use compound subjects in two sentences and circle the simple subjects. Use compound predicates in two sentences and circle the simple predicates.

1. _____

2. _____

3. _____

4. _____

Name _____

Compound sentences

Use **and** to combine two sentences when their thoughts complement each other.
Example: Saber-toothed tigers were prehistoric animals. They lived in Europe, Africa, and North and South America. Saber-toothed tigers were prehistoric animals, <u>and</u> they lived in Europe, Africa, and North and South America.

Use **but** to combine two sentences with contrasting thoughts.
Example: Saber-toothed tigers were carnivores. Elephants were herbivores.
Saber-toothed tigers were carnivores, <u>but</u> elephants were herbivores.

(Notice that the period at the end of each first sentence has been replaced with a comma, followed by *and* or *but*.)

Prehistoric Mammals

Combine each pair of sentences to write a compound sentence.

1. The first saber-toothed cats lived 40 million years ago. They became extinct about 10,000 years ago.

   _____

   _____

2. Saber-toothed tigers had large canine teeth. The 8-inch teeth were curved like swords.

   _____

   _____

3. They were carnivores. They ate thick-skinned animals like elephants and mastodons.

   _____

   _____

4. Prehistoric bears belonged to the carnivora family. Bears were also herbivores.

   _____

   _____

5. Mastodons were related to elephant-like animals. They were stockier and not as tall as elephants and mammoths.

   _____

   _____

Identifying complex sentences   Unit 4

A **complex sentence** contains an independent clause and one or more dependent clauses.

A **clause** is a group of words with a subject and a predicate. An **independent clause** can stand alone as a sentence.
Example: Most Aztecs were farmers. (This is both an independent clause and a sentence.)

A **dependent clause** cannot stand alone. It can function as a noun, an adjective, or an adverb.

A dependent clause that functions as a noun often begins with *that*.
Example: We learned <u>that most Aztecs were farmers</u>. (*We learned* is the independent clause. <u>That most Aztecs were farmers</u> is the dependent clause.)

A dependent clause that functions as an adjective often begins with *who, that, which, whom,* and *whose*. Example: The Aztecs <u>who were farmers</u> worked from dawn to dusk. (<u>Who were farmers</u> describes the noun Aztecs.)

A dependent clause that functions as an adverb tells where, when, or why an action occurred. Adverb clauses often begin with *after, when, where, while, wherever, because, since,* and *although*. Example: <u>Because they had no animals or plows</u>, the farmers' work was hard.

Down on the Farm, Aztec Style

Write **IC** if the sentence is an independent clause that stands alone. Write **X** to identify a complex sentence that contains one or more dependent clauses.

_____ 1. The Aztec farmers dug their fields by hand.

_____ 2. It was rich lake mud that made the fields so fertile.

_____ 3. The best fields, which were floating gardens, were in Lake Taxcoco.

_____ 4. Posts were hammered into the bottom of the lake.

_____ 5. Bundles of reeds and branches that were weighted with stones were sunk between the posts.

_____ 6. Mud was put on top of woven matting that was attached to the posts.

Underline the dependent clause in each of the following complex sentences.

7. Crops were planted in hanging gardens which were called chinampas.

8. Because they did not have cattle, the Aztecs mainly ate fruits and vegetables.

9. Maize, which was their main crop, was used to make flour for tortillas.

10. The women cooked the tortillas on round clay griddles that sat on three stones.

11. The Aztecs also made porridge from maize which was called atole.

12. They made tamales that were sometimes stuffed with snails or boiled grasshoppers.

Name

Read or listen to the directions. Fill in the circle beside the best answer.

 Example:

Which kind of sentence is this sentence?

Tell me why you are late.

(A) declarative   (B) interrogative

(C) imperative   (D) exclamatory

Answer: C because it is a command.

Now try these. You have 20 minutes.

Continue until you see ⬡STOP .

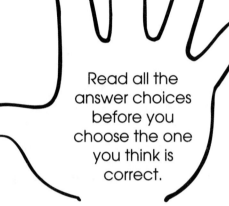

Read all the answer choices before you choose the one you think is correct.

---

1. Which sentence is a declarative sentence?

(A) Tell me about Diana Golden.   (B) Is Diana also a rock climber?

(C) She is a world champion skier.   (D) Golly, she is incredible!

---

2. Which sentence is an interrogative sentence?

(A) Diana began skiing as a child.

(B) Didn't she develop cancer when she was 12?

(C) Her cancerous right leg was removed.

(D) Oh, that is so sad!

---

3. Which sentence is not an exclamatory sentence?

(A) Goodness, Diana went on to ski on one leg!

(B) She must have worked and practiced very hard.

(C) Wow, she won three gold medals at the World Championships!

(D) Incredible, she is a true champion!

4. Which sentence is an imperative sentence?

(A) Diana was named U.S. Female Skier of the Year.

(B) Tell me what year she won that honor.

(C) Wasn't that in 1988?

(D) Yes, she was named by the U.S. Olympic Committee.

5. Why is this sentence an imperative sentence?

Hand in your report next Friday.

(A) It shows great emotion.   (B) It does not tell a complete thought.

(C) It asks a question.   (D) It gives a command.

6. Which is not a complete sentence?

(A) Sea anemones live on rocks in tide pools.

(B) Sometimes a sea anemone may look like a flower sprouting on a crab's back.

(C) Their tentacles have tiny stingers.

(D) Can paralyze shrimp, crabs, and snails.

7. Which is the simple subject of the sentence?

Different varieties of carnivorous plants live in North America.

Different	varieties	plants	live
(A)	(B)	(C)	(D)

8. Which is the simple predicate of the sentence?

Sundew plants trap insects by curling tightly around them.

trap	plants	curling	tightly
(A)	(B)	(C)	(D)

GO ON

Name

Which sentences in 9 and 10 have the complete subject underlined?

9. (A) The Pacific Ocean is the biggest ocean.

(B) The Pacific Ocean covers one-third of our planet.

(C) Over 25,000 islands are in the Pacific Ocean.

(D) The average depth of the Pacific Ocean is more than two miles.

10. (A) The Marianas Trench is Earth's deepest point.

(B) It is seven times deeper than the Grand Canyon.

(C) Strange creatures inhabit the depths of the oceans.

(D) Animals with body lights live in the deepest, darkest regions.

Which sentences in 11 and 12 have the complete predicates underlined?

11. (A) Scorpions use their pinchers to hold down their prey.

(B) The desert scorpion can live without water for three months.

(C) A scorpion carries venom in the tip of its tail.

(D) They have six to twelve eyes.

12. (A) False whip scorpions live in the tropics.

(B) They have eight long, thin legs.

(C) These fierce predators are not poisonous.

(D) They hunt at night and hide during the day.

Which sentences in 13 and 14 have compound subjects?

13. (A) No living things can survive at the exact North Pole.

(B) Birds and mammals can live in the surrounding areas, however.

(C) They have thick fur or feathers and thick layers of blubber.

(D) Some migrate to warmer places in the cold, dark winter months.

14. (A) Seals and penguins live in the seas around the South Pole.

(B) They feed on fish and squid.

(C) Blue whales visit both polar regions during their summers.

(D) The South Pole is covered with ice thousands of feet thick.

Which sentences in 15 and 16 have compound predicates?

15. (A) The La Brea tar pits are in Los Angeles, California.

(B) Prehistoric animals came to drink in a shallow pool and were trapped in the tar.

(C) About a million skeletons of prehistoric animals have been found in the tar pits.

(D) These pits are a rich source of Ice Age fossils.

16. (A) The first skeleton was found in the La Brea tar pits in 1906.

(B) Skeletons of saber-toothed tigers, camels, and horses have been recovered.

(C) Spanish settlers used the tar to waterproof adobe houses.

(D) Today, visitors come and visit a museum at the site.

Which sentence has both a compound subject and a compound predicate?

17. (A) New York City is famous for its architecture and skyscrapers.

(B) One of the oldest and most famous skyscrapers was completed in 1903.

(C) The Empire State Building and the RCA Building were both built in the 1930's.

(D) The Lever House and the United States Secretariat were designed and built since the 1950's.

GO ON

18. Which sentence is a compound sentence?

(A) Rudyard Kipling was a poet, novelist, and short-story writer.

(B) Kipling lived in India and England.

(C) He wrote realistic fiction, and he wrote fantasies.

(D) Kipling is remembered for writing <u>The Jungle Book</u> and "If-."

Which sentences in 19 and 20 are complex sentences?

19. (A) Seminole Indians who lived in the southeast were mostly farmers.

(B) They needed well-ventilated homes in the hot, steamy climate.

(C) The Seminoles lived on raised wood platforms with open sides and thatched roofs.

(D) The raised platforms kept the floor from rotting.

20. (A) The Iroquois, whose five tribes lived in the eastern woodlands, were farmers.

(B) These Native Americans were among the first to meet the European settlers.

(C) The settlers referred to the Iroquois as the "Five Nations."

(D) The Iroquois called themselves the "People of the Long House."

Write a compound sentence with either the conjunction **and** or **but**. Then write the reason why the conjunction you chose is correctly used in your sentence.

_____

_____

_____

_____

Midway Review Test Name Grid

Write your name in pencil in the boxes along the top. Begin with your last name. Fill in as many letters as will fit. Then follow the columns straight down and bubble in the letters that correspond with the letters in your name. Complete the rest of the information the same way. You may use a piece of scrap paper to help you keep your place.

STUDENT'S NAME		SCHOOL

LAST / FIRST / MI

TEACHER

FEMALE ○   MALE ○

DATE OF BIRTH

MONTH	DAY	YEAR
JAN ○	⓪ ⓪	⓪ ⓪
FEB ○	① ①	① ①
MAR ○	② ②	② ②
APR ○	③ ③	③ ③
MAY ○	④	④ ④
JUN ○	⑤	⑤ ⑤
JUL ○	⑥	⑥ ⑥
AUG ○	⑦	⑦ ⑦
SEP ○	⑧	⑧ ⑧
OCT ○	⑨	⑨ ⑨
NOV ○		
DEC ○		

GRADE ③   ④   ⑤

Name grid columns with bubbles A–Z for LAST, FIRST, and MI.

Midway Review Test Answer Sheet

Pay close attention when transferring your answers. Fill in the bubbles neatly and completely. You may use a piece of scrap paper to help you keep your place.

SAMPLES
A Ⓐ Ⓑ Ⓒ Ⓓ
B Ⓕ Ⓖ Ⓗ Ⓙ

1 Ⓐ Ⓑ Ⓒ Ⓓ   7 Ⓐ Ⓑ Ⓒ Ⓓ   13 Ⓐ Ⓑ Ⓒ Ⓓ   19 Ⓐ Ⓑ Ⓒ Ⓓ
2 Ⓕ Ⓖ Ⓗ Ⓙ   8 Ⓕ Ⓖ Ⓗ Ⓙ   14 Ⓕ Ⓖ Ⓗ Ⓙ   20 Ⓕ Ⓖ Ⓗ Ⓙ
3 Ⓐ Ⓑ Ⓒ Ⓓ   9 Ⓐ Ⓑ Ⓒ Ⓓ   15 Ⓐ Ⓑ Ⓒ Ⓓ
4 Ⓕ Ⓖ Ⓗ Ⓙ   10 Ⓕ Ⓖ Ⓗ Ⓙ   16 Ⓕ Ⓖ Ⓗ Ⓙ
5 Ⓐ Ⓑ Ⓒ Ⓓ   11 Ⓐ Ⓑ Ⓒ Ⓓ   17 Ⓐ Ⓑ Ⓒ Ⓓ
6 Ⓕ Ⓖ Ⓗ Ⓙ   12 Ⓕ Ⓖ Ⓗ Ⓙ   18 Ⓕ Ⓖ Ⓗ Ⓙ

Midway Review Test

Read or listen to the directions. Fill in the circle beside the best answer.

☐ Example:

Which sentence has a plural noun in the subject?

(A) Colonial women carded wool using carding paddles.

(B) Then the wool was spun into yarn.

(C) Finally, they wove the yarn into fabric on a loom.

(D) Flax and cotton were used to make cloth, also.

Answer: A because "Colonial women" is the subject. It tells what the sentence is about. "Women" is an irregular plural noun.

Remember your Helping Hand Strategies:

 1. Sometimes the correct answer is not given. Fill in the circle beside NG if no answer is correct.

 2. Always read each question carefully.

 3. Fill in the answer circles completely and neatly.

 4. Read all the answer choices before you choose the one you think is correct.

Now try these. You have 20 minutes. Continue until you see .

---

1. Which words are the common nouns in the following sentence?

Colonial people had to grow their own grain for bread.

(A) Colonial, people, grow
(B) people, grow, grain
(C) people, grain, bread
(D) grow, own, grain

---

2. Which sentence does not include a proper noun?

(F) Margaret Bourke-White was born in 1904 in New York City.

(G) She became a world-famous photographer.

(H) She took pictures for <u>Fortune</u> and <u>Life</u> magazines.

(J) Margaret was the first woman reporter for the U.S. Air Force.

 GO ON

Name _____

3. Which word is not an abstract noun?

    conscience   pride   apathy   lyrics

       (A)   (B)   (C)   (D)

4. Which sentence has a possessive noun?

(F) Arthur's going to meet me at the library.

(G) He is doing research for a project in Mr. Ryan's class.

(H) Arthur wants me to help him with his project.

(J) I can't help him until tomorrow.

5. Which word is the collective noun in the sentence?

A pod of whales swam along the California coast.

    pod   whales   California   coast

    (A)   (B)   (C)   (D)

6. Which sentence contains a reflexive pronoun?

(F) Joel's baseball coach showed him how to properly slide into the base.

(G) The coach did not want Joel to hurt himself.

(H) Joel and his teammates practiced different sliding techniques.

(J) Joel slid correctly into third base in his next game.

7. Which sentence has a future tense verb?

(A) Bonnie took a spelling test Tuesday.

(B) She said she thought she did well.

(C) Bonnie is anxious to get the test results.

(D) She will check with her teacher tomorrow.

8. Choose the correct possessive pronoun for the underlined words.

Children and adults like <u>Jack Prelutsky's</u> funny poems.

    him   his   their   NG
    (F)   (G)   (H)   (J)

9. Which sentence has a present perfect tense verb?

(A) The scientist has visited Tasmania before.

(B) He saw an unusual mammal called a platypus.

(C) It had webbed feet and a bill like a duck.

(D) He said female platypuses lay eggs.

10. Which answer is the present progressive tense of **watch**?

    watches   is watching   has watched   watched
    (F)   (G)   (H)   (J)

11. Which word is an adjective in the sentence?

A loris is a primate with powerful hands and feet.

    loris   primate   powerful   feet
    (A)   (B)   (C)   (D)

12. Which word is a proper adjective in the sentence?

Lorises live in southern India and Southeast Asia.

    Lorises   India   Asia   NG
    (F)   (G)   (H)   (J)

13. Identify the adverb in the sentence.

A male proboscis monkey's nose grows continuously throughout his life.

    proboscis   grows   continuously   life
    (A)   (B)   (C)   (D)

GO ON ▷

Midway Review Test

14. Which sentence does not contain a prepositional phrase?

(F) Charles Lindbergh made the first solo flight across the Atlantic Ocean.

(G) His historic flight was made in 1927.

(H) He landed outside Paris, France.

(J) He instantly became a hero and a celebrity.

15. Which sentence contains a coordinating conjunction?

(A) Amelia Earhart took her first flying lessons in 1921.

(B) She bought her first airplane and set the women's altitude record in 1922.

(C) Amelia became the first woman to fly solo across the Atlantic Ocean in 1932.

(D) She also set the women's transcontinental speed record in the same year.

16. Which sentence has the complete subject underlined?

(F) The human body is about 60 percent water.

(G) Human, plant, and animal life would be impossible without water.

(H) Some plants and animals can store water until they need it.

(J) Other living things spend their entire lives in fresh or salt water.

17. Which sentence has the complete predicate underlined?

(A) Plants take in water through their roots.

(B) Water travels to the stems, leaves, and flowers of the plant.

(C) Water leaves plants through tiny holes in their leaves called stomata.

(D) Water is released by humans through holes in their skin called pores.

Name

18. Which sentence has a compound predicate?

(F) Zebus are cattle with large shoulder humps.

(G) They have flaps of skin hanging from their throats.

(H) Zebus are sacred animals to the Hindus in India.

(J) Zebus pull plows and turn gristmills for non-Hindus, however.

19. Which sentence is a compound sentence?

(A) The great horned owl hunts at night and kills instantly.

(B) It is a fierce hunter, and it uses its eyes and ears to locate food.

(C) The owl glides silently before making a lightning-strike dive for its prey.

(D) Its feet have four toes with razor-sharp talons to grab an animal.

20. Which sentence is a complex sentence?

(F) Benjamin Franklin was born in 1706 into a very large family.

(G) He had 16 brothers and sisters.

(H) Ten-year-old Benjamin Franklin worked in his father's business.

(J) After two years, Ben went to work for his brother who was a printer.

Write an interrogative sentence with a past tense irregular verb.

_____

_____

_____

_____

Name

First word of a sentence, quotation, and I

The **first word of a sentence** and a **quotation** begins with a capital letter. The pronoun **I** is always a capital letter.

Examples: "<u>I</u> would like to know how astronauts dress when they walk in space," said Monroe. (<u>I</u> is the first word of a sentence, the first word of a quotation, and the pronoun *I*.)

Acid Rain

Read each sentence. Write **yes** if the sentence has the correct capitalization. Write **no** if it does not.

_____ 1. "The acidity level in rain is increasing," said Helen's teacher, Mr. Nash.

_____ 2. "what causes the increase in acidity?" asked the girl.

_____ 3. Mr. Hill answered, "pollution from cars and factories causes acid rain."

_____ 4. "Actually, snow, hail, fog, and mist can contain harmful acids, also."

_____ 5. "Acid rain can damage plants and animals," continued the teacher.

_____ 6. Helen said, "I read that our health can be affected by acid rain."

_____ 7. "that's true, Helen, but humans cause most of the pollution."

_____ 8. "When pollution is carried into the atmosphere, it will fall as rain or snow at some time," explained Mr. Hill.

Use the proofreading mark to show where each capital letter is needed.

9. "automobiles emit poisonous gases," continued Helen's teacher.

10. Helen said, "i think power plants and oil refineries must cause pollution, too."

11. "yes, they emit a lot of sulfur dioxide and nitrogen oxides."

12. Mr. Hill said, "erupting volcanoes spew sulfur dioxide into the atmosphere."

Rewrite each sentence below on another sheet of paper. Use capital letters where they are needed.

13. "weather conditions affect how far pollutants travel," said Mr. Hill.

14. "britain's acid rain can fall in Scandinavian countries."

15. Mr. Hill said, "trees in those countries are being harmed by acid rain."

Names of persons and family members
Unit 5

The **first**, **middle**, and **last** names of persons begin with capital letters. Example: A̲my L̲ee D̲avis

N̲ames of **family members** begin with capital letters when they are used as proper nouns.
Examples: G̲randma, A̲unt J̲o E̲llen, C̲ousin S̲ol (N̲ote: Do not capitalize them when they are used as common nouns, such as my grandma, her aunt, his cousin.)

A Capital Idea

Write **yes** if the names of the persons and family members
are written correctly. Write **no** if they are not.

_____ 1. Kevin sherwin

_____ 2. aunt Rosie

_____ 3. Curtis Joe Bambrick

_____ 4. Emily Wood

_____ 5. Uncle Ramon

_____ 6. Granny Mo

_____ 7. Angela ann Pate

_____ 8. Grandfather Todd

Tallulah Louise

Write the names of persons and family members correctly.

9. betty and brett breeze

_____

10. carl edward smith

_____

11. uncle richard

_____

12. grandmother rebecca

_____

13. collin o'keefe

_____

14. auntie louise

_____

Write each sentence correctly.

15. Why don't uncle marvin and aunt susan meet us at the restaurant?

_____

16. albert, barry, and sammie will be there, too.

_____

17. We'll have fun celebrating grandma's and grandpa's fiftieth wedding anniversary.

_____

Titles of respect and initials

Titles of respect begin with capital letters. Most are used in front of the person's name.
Jr. and Sr. follow some men's names. Examples: <u>M</u>r. (man), <u>M</u>rs. (married woman),
<u>M</u>s. (married or unmarried woman), <u>M</u>iss (unmarried woman or girl), <u>D</u>r. (doctor),
and <u>R</u>ev. (Reverend)

Example: <u>M</u>s. Rosa Parks was born in Tuskegee, Alabama.

An **initial** is the first letter of a person's name. It is always a capital letter.
Example: Ms. <u>R</u>. Parks attended Alabama State Teachers College.

Paying Respect

Write each name correctly.

1. dr. ronald j. lohmar

_____

2. ms. s. p. steed

_____

3. miss stacy justus

_____

4. mr. and mrs. garcia

_____

Write each sentence correctly.

5. In 1955, rosa parks, an African-American woman, was arrested in Montgomery, Alabama.

_____

6. ms. parks had refused to give up her seat on a city bus to a white person.

_____

7. ms. jo ann robinson and mr. e. d. nixon led a boycott of the buses.

_____

8. dwight d. eisenhower was president of the United States at the time.

_____

Names of places (streets, cities, states, and their abbreviations)

Unit 5

Names of streets and their **abbreviations** begin with capital letters. There may be more than one word in the name. Examples: <u>O</u>ak <u>F</u>orest <u>P</u>arkway, <u>T</u>owerwood <u>Dr</u>., <u>H</u>armony <u>Ln</u>.

Names of cities and states begin with capital letters. There may be more than one word in the name. **Two-letter postal abbreviations** for states are capitalized.

Return to Sender

Write each address correctly as a return address on an envelope.

1. 2148 serena pl.
   oakland, ca 94601

   _____

   _____

2. 5234 autumn avenue
   bristol, ny 14469

   _____

   _____

3. 17591 liberty trail dr.
   deer park, illinois 60010

   _____

   _____

4. 8820 e. pacific st.
   stony ridge, indiana 46538

   _____

   _____

5. 4224 brookstone terrace
   wildwood, ky 40223

   _____

   _____

6. 94 sun lake st.
   bruin, pennsylvania 16022

   _____

   _____

Charlie Hall
140 Mayberry St.
Grove, Ohio 44042

Miss Carol Hardy
8321 Laurel Road
St. Louis, Mo. 63043

Write each sentence correctly on another sheet of paper.

7. Did Boyd move from atlanta, georgia, to rock creek, maryland?

8. Shelly lives at 76 miller forest road in summit city, michigan.

9. My grandmother's address is 23 carriage crossing lane.

10. She lives in florence, nebraska, and my family lives in fort morgan, colorado.

Name

Names of places and things   Unit 5

Names of nations, continents, and certain **parts or regions** of nations and continents begin with capital letters. Examples: Germany (nation), Africa (continent), South Pole (region)

Names of specific and **special oceans, lakes, rivers, islands,** and such, begin with capital letters. Examples: Atlantic Ocean, Mississippi River, Long Island

Names of special buildings, structures, and **places** begin with capital letters. Examples: Sunset School, Golden Gate Bridge, Forest Park

Names of days of the week and **months of the year** begin with capital letters. Examples: Sunday, July

Names of holidays and **special days** begin with capital letters. Example: Thanksgiving Day

Names of organizations, institutions, and **companies** begin with capital letters. There may be more than one word in the name. Words like *and* and *of* are not capitalized. Examples: Girls Scouts of America, University of Michigan, Quack & Company, Inc.

Names of special events begin with capital letters. Example: Kentucky Derby

Especially Special

Write each sentence correctly.

1. Toby's class studied england during multicultural week at bingham school.

2. Some students made a replica of the tower of london.

3. Others drew pictures of buckingham palace and westminster abbey.

4. Toby learned that northern ireland, scotland, wales, and england together make up the united kingdom.

5. Jamar visited the smithsonian institution in washington, d. c. last wednesday.

6. Kyle attended the new york philharmonic concert april 6.

7. This year, christmas eve and the first day of hanukkah both fall on a monday.

Friendly letters and business letters — Unit 5

Friendly letters and **business letters** differ in their purposes, but the same capitalization rules apply to both types of letters. In addition to the five parts of a friendly letter—the heading, the greeting, the body of the letter, the closing, and the name—a business letter has an inside address, and a signature.

The first word and proper nouns in the greeting begin with capital letters.
Example of a greeting for a friendly letter: Dear Mom and Dad,
Example of a greeting for a business letter: Dear Toy Palace:
(Note: A colon is used after the greeting of a business letter instead of a comma.)

The first word of the closing begins with a capital letter. Example of a closing for a friendly letter: Love, Example of a closing for a business letter: Sincerely yours,

Special Delivery

Use the proofreading mark to show where each capital letter is needed in the friendly letter.

6844 lone elk lane
fox lake, minnesota 56181
august 1, 2001

dear grandma and grandpa,

dad and i returned from our fishing trip last night. we really had a great time, even though we did not catch many fish. we plan to try again in the fall.

love,
brenda

Use the proofreading mark to show where each capital letter is needed in the business letter.

1798 florence street
sunny slopes, indiana 47401
february 20, 2002

ms. roberta jones, president
simply seeds, inc.
box 77
baldwin, georgia 30511

dear ms. jones:

please send me your seed catalog to the address above as soon as possible. i want to purchase some of your tomato seeds to grow in my hothouse.

sincerely,
albert armstrong
albert armstrong

Outline form

An **outline** is useful to use for writing a **report**. It contains information taken from notes made about the subject of the report.

The first word, the last word, and the important words in the topic and each main idea begin with capital letters. The first word of each supporting idea begins with a capital letter.

Writing an Outline

Study the example of an outline below. Notice the use of Roman numerals for main ideas and capital letters for supporting ideas.

The Early Life of John Adams

I. John Adam's Childhood
    A. Born in Braintree, Massachusetts, 1735
    B. Father—a farmer, church deacon, and militia officer
    C. Mother—from family of merchants and physicians
    D. Went to the village school and worked on the farm

II. Education
    A. Graduated from Harvard College
    B. Taught school a short time
    C. Studied law and began to practice law in 1758
    D. Moved to Boston and became a leading
       attorney for the Massachusetts colony

III. Adam's Family
    A. Married Abigail Smith in 1764
    B. Had five children

Use the proofreading mark to show where each capital letter is needed in the outline below.

John Adam's Early Political Career

I. in new england
    a. protested the Stamp Act of 1765
    b. elected to represent Boston in the colonial legislature
    c. defended colonists' actions at the Boston Tea Party

II. national politics
    a. massachusetts delegate to the First Continental Congress in 1774
    b. persuaded Congress to organize Continental Army
    c. served as chairman of the Continental Board of War and Ordnance
    d. a signer of the Declaration of Independence
    e. wrote almost all of the Massachusetts Constitution of 1780

77

Book and magazine titles and titles of works   Unit 5

Begin the first word, the last word, and each important word in the **title of a book** or **magazine** with a capital letter. Example: Lost in Cyberspace (Lost is the first word of the book title. Cyberspace is the last word. *In* is not an important word in the title and should not be capitalized.)

Underline the title of a book or magazine when it is in a sentence.
Example: Daughters is a magazine title.

Begin the first word, the last word, and each important word in the **titles of stories**, **articles**, **poems**, **songs**, **movies**, and **television programs** with capital letters. Quotation marks are used around these titles.

Examples: "Master of All Masters" (story), "The Big Open" (article), "I Never Saw a Moor" (poem), "Scarborough Fair" (song), "King Kong" (movie), "I Love Lucy" (television program)

Bestsellers

Write each sentence correctly. Remember: underline book and magazine titles in sentences.

1. Jill wanted to check out julie of the wolves, but it was not available.

   _____

2. Then the librarian helped her find little house on the prairie.

   _____

3. John enjoyed reading scientific american explorations.

   _____

4. He would like a subscription to national geographic for his birthday.

   _____

Use the proofreading mark to show where each capital letter is needed in the titles of stories, articles, poems, and songs.

5. Robert Louis Stevenson wrote the poem "the happy thought."

6. "flower spiders" is an article about spiders that prey on insects that pollinate flowers.

7. "you're a grand old flag" is a patriotic song.

8. "little one-inch" is a Japanese tale.

9. "a bug's life" was a popular movie.

10. Have you ever seen "angela anaconda" on television?

Write a paragraph using six different capitalization rules.

Name

Unit 5 Test

Mechanics: Capitalization

Read or listen to the directions. Fill in the circle beside the best answer.

⬜ Example:

Which word or words should not begin with capital letters?

(A) Uncle   (B) Grandma Rita

(C) Aunt Anna   (D) Ms. Frost

Answer: A because **uncle** is not a proper noun.

Now try these. You have 20 minutes. Continue until you see ⬡STOP .

Cross out answers you know are wrong.

---

1. Which sentence is written correctly?

(A) i never knew that Benjamin Franklin invented a clock.

(B) Dad and i read that it was the first clock to show hours, minutes, and seconds.

(C) previous clocks only showed the hours and minutes.

(D) I think Benjamin Franklin was an amazing person.

---

2. Which quotation is not written correctly?

(A) "What are some things that Benjamin Franklin is noted for?" asked Ms. Kane.

(B) "Benjamin Franklin wrote <u>Poor Richard's Almanac</u>," answered Jason.

(C) Maria asked, "wasn't he an inventor, too?"

(D) "Yes, he invented the lightning rod," replied Ms. Kane.

---

3. Which title of respect and name is not written correctly?

(A) Ms. Andrea tillis   (B) Mr. Arnold Skelly

(C) Miss Molly McRea   (D) Dr. B. Rimmins

---

4. Which street name is written correctly?

(A) 72 country Acres Lane

(B) 4049 Cambridge ct.

(C) 5443 nothingham dr.

(D) 1157 Wakeshire Ter.

5. Which city and state is written correctly?

(A) Fox Ridge, indiana

(B) west Haven, Connecticut

(C) Grand Isle, NE

(D) Grand rapids, MI

6. Which sentence is not written correctly?

(A) Is Mt. Everest in nepal?

(B) The Ganges is a river in India.

(C) The Hawaiian Islands are in the Pacific Ocean.

(D) Crete is an island in the Mediterranean Sea.

7. Which sentence is written correctly?

(A) The Panama Canal connects two Oceans.

(B) The Sahara desert stretches across Africa.

(C) Marrakech is an ancient city in Morocco.

(D) The Capital of Australia is Canberra.

8. Which sentence is not written correctly?

(A) Jana's birthday is on the Fourth of July.

(B) That's another name for Independence Day.

(C) Isn't your birthday on halloween?

(D) Yes, my birthday is October 31.

Unit 5 Test

9. Which sentence is written correctly?

(A) Have you ever been to the Strawberry Festival?

(B) The girl scouts have an annual food collection in our town.

(C) Memorial day is always the fourth Monday in May.

(D) We do not have school on Martin luther King Day.

10. Which greeting of a friendly letter is written correctly?

(A) Dear roy and karen,

(B) Dear Aunt Sue and Tony

(C) Dear Sir:

(D) NG

11. Which line of the heading is not correct?

(A) 1941 Bamberry Blvd.

(B) Cool Spring, South Carolina 29511

(C) august 29, 2000

(D) NG

12. Which closing of a business letter is correct?

Love,	Your Friend,	Sincerely yours,	Sincerely Yours,
(A)	(B)	(C)	(D)

13. Which main idea in an outline is written correctly?

(A) I. Heating with Water

(B) II. Cooling with water

(C) III. electricity from water

(D) IV. Water In The Air

GO ON

14. Which sentence is written correctly?

(A) Sophia's book report was on <u>Horses in The Garage</u>.

(B) Sophia's book report was on <u>Horses In The Garage</u>.

(C) Sophia's book report was on <u>Horses in the Garage</u>.

(C) Sophia's book report was on <u>Horses in the garage</u>.

15. Which magazine title is written correctly?

(A) Please save your copy of <u>Sports illustrated for Kids</u>.

(B) Please save your copy of <u>Sports Illustrated for Kids</u>.

(C) Please save your copy of <u>Sports Illustrated For Kids</u>.

(D) Please save your copy of <u>Sports Illustrated For kids</u>.

16. Which sentence is written correctly?

(A) "The four Musicians" is an old folk tale.

(B) "Pied Piper Of Hamelin" is a story from Germany.

(C) A favorite African folk tale is "The fire on the Mountain."

(D) "The Taming of the Shrew" was based on a folk tale.

17. Which title of a poem is written correctly?

(A) "Something told the wild Geese"

(B) "A Charm For Spring Flowers"

(C) "Yesterday in Oxford Street"

(D) "The snow man"

Unit 5 Test

18. Which sentence is not written correctly?

(A) Did Toni sing "The Star-Spangled Banner" at the assembly?

(B) No, she sang "America The Beautiful."

(C) Noah sang "This Land Is Your Land."

(D) The entire class sang "A Grand Old Flag."

19. Which sentence is written correctly?

(A) Troy and I saw "The lion king" at the theater.

(B) Troy liked "Recess: School's Out" better.

(C) I liked it better than "Atlantis, The Lost Empire."

(D) My favorite movie is "The Parent trap."

20. Which sentence is not written correctly?

(A) Samantha watches "Nickelodeon."

(B) Sometimes she watches "Two of a Kind" on television.

(C) She also enjoys watching "Boy Meets World."

(D) She hardly ever watches "The brothers Garcia."

Explain the difference between the capitalization of a main idea and the capitalization of a supporting detail in an outline.

_____

_____

_____

_____

Periods for declarative, imperative, and compound sentences   Unit 6

A **declarative sentence** tells a complete idea. It ends with a period (.).
Example: Walt Disney began his career making short films.

An **imperative sentence** gives an order. It ends with a period (.).
Example: Tell me what the first short films were.

A **compound sentence** combines two sentences. It ends with a period (.).
Example: They were called "Laugh-O-Grams," and he made these with another man, Ub Iwerks.

Mickey and Friends

Identify each sentence and add a period. Write **D** for declarative sentences, **I** for imperative sentences, and **C** for compound sentences.

_____ 1. Walt and Ub left Kansas in 1923, and they went to Hollywood

_____ 2. They produced two animated film series there

_____ 3. Tell me the names of the two series

_____ 4. One was "Alice in Cartoonland," and the other was "Oswald the Rabbit"

_____ 5. The two cartoonists became famous when they created a black-and-white mouse

_____ 6. Let me guess; that must have been Mickey Mouse

_____ 7. Yes, Mickey first appeared in a silent film, "Plane Crazy," in 1928

_____ 8. Mickey was an instant success, and all ages loved the mischievous little mouse

_____ 9. He was given a voice in "Steamboat Willie"

_____ 10. Soon Walt and Ub created Minnie Mouse, Donald Duck, Pluto, and Goofy

Write each sentence correctly on another sheet of paper.

11. Walt and Ub produced the first Technicolor cartoon in 1932

12. Disney made the first full-length cartoon feature in 1937

13. Name that film for me

14. It was "Snow White and the Seven Dwarfs"

Periods for titles of respect, initials, and abbreviations — Unit 6

Use a period after a **title of respect**, such as Mr., Mrs., Ms., and Dr., and a person's initials. (Do not use a period after Miss.) Examples: Mr. Grundy, Dr. Meitz, R. W. Wall

Use a period after an **abbreviation**. (Do not use a period after two-letter postal abbreviations such as NY and OR.) Examples: Junior/Jr., Tuesday/Tues., Drive/Dr.

Powerful Punctuation!

Write each name correctly.

1. Ms Paula Shannon

   _____

2. Mr John W Weiler

   _____

3. Miss Barbara J Rizzo

   _____

4. Rev and Mrs Handley

   _____

5. Mrs R S Streeter

   _____

6. Dr Thomas L Hutson

   _____

7. Patrick Markham, Sr

   _____

8. Mr and Mrs Storey

   _____

Write the correct abbreviation for each word.

9. Street _____

10. Thursday _____

11. Junior _____

12. December _____

13. Avenue _____

14. Drive _____

15. The Reverend _____

16. Doctor _____

Use the proofreading mark to show where each period should be added in the note below. ⊙

Date: Aug 29, 2001
To: Mr Robert H Samuels
From: Ms Freeman

Dr Evans' secretary called to remind you of your appointment on Wed, Sept 4 at 3:00. Please call his office if you cannot keep this appointment.

Just a note ^
Bobby,
Ben called. He wants you and Sam to come to his birthday party on Sat. May 1st.
Mom

Periods in outline form

Unit 6

When writing an **outline**, use periods after Roman numerals for main ideas. Use periods after capital letters for supporting details.

This Is About Outlines, Period!

Study the example of an outline below.

Cactus

I. Life Cycle of the Cactus
   - A. Reproduce by pollination
   - B. Produce fruit with seeds
   - C. Grow very slowly
   - D. Live from 50 to 200 years
II. Common Kinds of Cactuses
   - A. Organ pipe cactuses
   - B. Barrel cactuses
   - C. Saguaro cactuses
III. The Importance of Cactuses
   - A. Food for animals, birds, and insects
   - B. Food for people
   - C. Sell as a product

Use the proofreading mark to show where each period is needed in the outline below.

African Rain forests

I Plants in African Rain forests

   A Fewer plants than in South American rain forests

   B 50 to 100 species of trees, including valuable woods like ebony

   C Oil palms and coffee plants

II Animals in African Rain forests

   A Large variety of animals

   B Monkeys and birds in the canopy and sub-canopy

   C Wild hogs, mandrills, and okapi on the ground

   D Gorillas and chimpanzees on the ground and in trees

III People of the African Rain forests

   A Pygmies in the forests

   B Hunt wild animals and gather plants

Question marks and exclamation marks

An **interrogative sentence** asks a question. Use a question mark (**?**) at the end of the sentence. Example: What is an avalanche?

An **exclamatory sentence** shows great emotion. Use an exclamation mark (**!**) at the end of an exclamatory sentence. An exclamatory sentence often begins or ends with an interjection such as wow. Example: Wow, look out for the avalanche!

Avalanche!

Identify each sentence. Write **I** for interrogative sentence. Write **E** for exclamatory sentence. Add the correct punctuation at the end of each sentence.

_____ 1. Is an avalanche a huge mass of ice and snow

_____ 2. Does the mass break away from the side of a mountain

_____ 3. Goodness, the worst avalanches occur in the Alps

_____ 4. What are the three kinds of avalanches

_____ 5. Wow, the force of a dry-snow avalanche can equal that of a hurricane

_____ 6. That's unbelievable

_____ 7. Do wet-snow avalanches usually happen in the spring

_____ 8. Oh my, the wet snow forms into huge boulders rolling down the mountain

_____ 9. Good grief, the wet snow can become as hard as concrete

_____ 10. Is the third kind called a slab avalanche

Write the sentences below on another sheet of paper. Add the correct punctuation.

11. Can noises cause avalanches

12. Do you mean that a clap of thunder can start an avalanche

13. That's hard to believe

14. Well, you won't believe this either

15. Are you saying that even the falling of an icicle can set off an avalanche

Commas in dates, city and states, and in letters   Unit 6

Use a comma (,) to separate the **day** from the **year**. Also, use a comma after the year if it is not last in a sentence. Example: March 31, 1995, was the date on which Juan was born.

Use a comma to separate the name of **city** from a **state**. Also, use a comma after the name of the state if it is not last in a sentence. Example: Topeka, Kansas, was Juan's birthplace.

Use a comma after the **greeting** of a friendly letter and after the **closing** of both a friendly letter and a business letter. Examples: Dear Juan, (greeting) Yours truly, (closing)

Common Commas

Write the dates, cities and states, greetings, and closings correctly.

1. North Oaks California

   _____

2. Halawa Hills HA

   _____

3. December 21 2000

   _____

4. Dear Uncle Harvey

   _____

5. Your cousin

   _____

6. July 18 2001

   _____

7. Colony Park Georgia

   _____

8. Dear Mom and Dad

   _____

Use the proofreading mark to show where each comma is needed in the friendly letter below.   ⌃

> 1476 Sixth Street
> Magnolia Springs Maryland 20784
> February 3 2001

Dear Ronnie

    I was happy to hear you will be in town next Wednesday February 8. I hope I can see you before I leave for Canton Ohio on the 9th. Please call when you get into town.

> Your friend
> Wally

Name

Lights, Camera, Action!

Are the colons and commas used correctly in the sentences? Write **yes** or **no** on the line.

_____ 1. Here are some child stars of the early movies: Shirley Temple, Jackie Cooper, and Margaret O'Brien.

_____ 2. Mickey Rooney, Judy Garland and Clark Gable starred in musicals in the 1930's.

_____ 3. The following were big Hollywood stars in the late 1950's: Marlon Brando, James Dean, and Paul Newman.

_____ 4. Harrison Ford starred in action films of the 1980's such as "Raiders of the Lost Ark," "Indiana Jones and the Temple of Doom," and "Indiana Jones and the Last Crusade."

_____ 5. These were films for family viewing in the 1990's: "Honey, I Shrunk the Kids" "The Secret Garden" and "Mrs. Doubtfire."

Use proofreading marks to show where colons and/or commas are needed in each sentence.   ⊙ ⌃

6. Some of the earliest jungle films are as follows "Tarzan the Ape Man" "King Kong" and "Tarzan and His Mate."

7. "Animal Crackers" "Monkey Business" and "Horse Feathers" were made by the Marx Brothers in the 1930's.

8. Harpo Chico and Groucho Marx made many more silly slapstick films.

9. Older generations will remember these Jerry Lewis' films "The Bellboy" "The Nutty Professor" and "The Disorderly Orderly."

 On another sheet of paper, write a sentence using a colon and commas to describe three or more movies or movie stars you like.

Commas with nouns of address, interjections, and interrupters   Unit 6

Use a comma (,) to set apart all **nouns of address** in a sentence. Examples: *Tamika,* did you know that the Gateway Arch is the tallest monument in the world? Did you know, *class,* that the Gateway Arch is the tallest monument in the world? Did you know that the Gateway Arch is the tallest monument in the world, *children*?

Use a comma after words like **yes** or **no**, or after mild **interjections** at the beginning of a sentence. Example: *No,* I didn't know that. *Well,* it's true.

Use a comma to separate words that **interrupt** the thought of the sentence from the rest of the sentence. *Therefore, however, after all, currently,* and *consequently* are examples of adverbs that act as interrupters. Example: The Gateway Arch is, *after all,* 630 feet tall.

Little, but Mighty

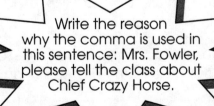

Use the proofreading mark to show where each comma is needed in the sentences.

1. Please tell me more about the Gateway Arch Mrs. Fowler.

2. Well it is made of stainless steel.

3. The legs are hollow so consequently small elevators can go up to the top.

4. The Arch is in St. Louis on the Mississippi River Tamika.

5. Mrs. Fowler isn't the San Jacinto Monument the tallest column in the world?

6. Yes you are correct Tamika.

7. The column is 571 feet tall class and it has a 220-ton star on top.

8. Goodness that must be an impressive sight to see.

9. Yes particularly when you consider it was built in 1936.

10. Show the class this picture of the column Tamika.

11. Children has anyone visited Mount Rushmore in South Dakota?

12. Currently Mount Rushmore is the largest completed sculpture in the world.

13. However a 564-foot statue is being carved that will be taller than Mount Rushmore.

14. It is a statue of Chief Crazy Horse students.

Write the reason why the comma is used in this sentence: Mrs. Fowler, please tell the class about Chief Crazy Horse.

Commas with appositives and compound sentences   Unit 6

Use commas to separate an **appositive** that immediately follows a noun from the rest of the sentence. An appositive is a word or phrase that explains or identifies a noun.
Example: The Arkansas River, *one of the main tributaries of the Mississippi,* begins in the Rocky Mountains. (The phrase, *one of the main tributaries of the Mississippi,* identifies the Arkansas River. Without the phrase, the reader may not know that it is a tributary.)

Use a comma before the word *and* to separate the two parts of a **compound sentence**.
Example: The Arkansas River flows from Colorado, *and* it empties into the Mississippi in Arkansas.

America's Waterways

Use the proofreading mark to show where each comma is needed in the sentences.

1. The Arkansas River flows through a deep canyon the Royal Gorge in Colorado.

2. It flows through Tulsa the largest city on the river before reaching Little Rock.

3. The Colorado River the longest river west of the Rocky Mountains empties into the Gulf of California.

4. The Colorado River has cut deep canyons into rock and one of these canyons is the Grand Canyon.

5. The Grand Canyon is 277 miles long and it is more than a mile deep.

6. Hoover Dam the largest dam on the Colorado is on the border of Arizona and Nevada.

7. The word "Mississippi" an Algonquian Indian word means "father of waters."

8. The Mississippi a 2,340-mile-long river is truly the "father of waters."

9. It is the main river drainage system in America and it drains an area of 1.2 million square miles.

10. The country's longest river the Missouri is called "The Big Muddy" because it carries so much sediment.

Read the sentence. Write the reasons the commas are used in the sentence.

The Rio Grande River, Spanish for "great river," forms the border between Texas and Mexico, and it empties into the Gulf of Mexico.

_____

_____

Name

Commas and quotation marks in dialogue   Unit 6

When two or more people are talking, they are having a conversation. A **dialogue** is the conversation in written form. Use quotation marks (" ") around the spoken words.

The **speaker's tag** tells who is speaking. Use a comma (,) after the speaker's tag when it begins a sentence.

Example: Tony asked, "What are you looking at through the telescope?"
        (speaker's tag)   (dialogue)

Use a comma (,) after the spoken words and before the quotation marks (" ") when the speaker's tag is at the end of a sentence. (Note: If the sentence ends with a question mark or an exclamation mark, do not use a comma.)

Example: "I'm looking at a constellation," answered Dr. Tan, an astronomer.
          (dialogue)   (speaker's tag)

Orion, the Mighty Hunter

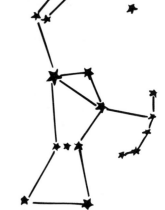

Write the sentences. Use quotation marks and commas correctly.

1. Tony asked What constellation do you see?

   _____

   _____

2. I see Orion, which is a winter constellation answered the astronomer.

   _____

3. Dr. Tan continued That means it is visible only from late October until April.

   _____

4. Orion has more bright stars than other constellations explained Dr. Tan.

   _____

5. The astronomer said Here, Tony, look through the telescope.

   _____

6. Can you find the three bright stars in a row? asked Dr. Tan.

   _____

7. Those stars represent Orion's belt, and the dimmer ones are his shield he said.

   _____

Name _____

Quotation marks with titles of works
Unit 6

Use quotation marks around titles of **stories**, **articles**, **poems**, **songs**, **movies**, and **television programs**. Examples: "March and the Shepherd" (story), "In the Shadow of the Andes" (article), "My Heart's in the Highlands" (poem), "102 Dalmations" (movie), "The Jetsons" (television program)

Remarkable Quotation Marks

Write the story titles correctly.

1. The King of the Mountain

   _____

2. The Mice That Ate Iron

   _____

Write the article titles correctly.

5. Rebirth of an Urban Prairie

   _____

6. End of the Line

   _____

Write the poem titles correctly.

9. Loveliest of Trees

   _____

10. There Will Come Soft Rains

    _____

Write the television program titles correctly.

11. Kids from Room 402

    _____

12. Family Matters

    _____

Write the song titles correctly.

3. Home on the Range

   _____

4. Give My Regards to Broadway

   _____

Write the movie titles correctly.

7. Hercules

   _____

8. Free Willy

   _____

The Wild Pony

Apostrophes in contractions and possessive nouns   Unit 6

An **apostrophe** (') is used in place of the letter or letters left out in a **contraction**.
Many contractions are made by joining linking verbs and the word *not*.
Example: do not/<u>don't</u> (An apostrophe takes the place of the *o* in *not*.)

Some contractions are made by joining pronouns and verbs. An apostrophe (') is used in
place of the letter or letters left out. Example: we are/<u>we're</u> (An apostrophe takes the
place of the *a* in *are*.)

Add an **apostrophe** and **–s** (**'s**) to most singular common and proper nouns to show
possession. Add an apostrophe (') to most common and proper plural nouns to show
possession. Add an apostrophe and **–s** (**'s**) to irregular plural nouns to show possession.
Examples: the book<u>'s</u> title, the storie<u>s'</u> illustrators, the people<u>'s</u> favorite poems

Let's Read!

Write the contraction for each pair of words.

1. he would   _____   2. will not   _____

3. should not _____   4. they will   _____

5. story is   _____   6. Harriet is _____

Rewrite each phrase, using a possessive noun for each underlined noun.
Example: the viewpoint of the <u>author</u>/the <u>author's</u> viewpoint

7. the book of <u>Richard Peek</u>   _____

8. the illustrations of <u>Donald Small</u>   _____

9. the biography of <u>Abraham Lincoln</u>   _____

Each of the following sentences contains a word with an apostrophe. Write **C** if the
word with the apostrophe is a contraction. Write **PN** if it is a possessive noun.

_____ 10. Allen Say's illustrations for <u>Grandfather's Journal</u> won the Caldecott Medal.

_____ 11. Didn't he received that award in 1999?

_____ 12. Yes, it was Mr. Say's first Caldecott Medal.

_____ 13. Chris Van Allburg's illustrations have been honored twice.

_____ 14. Well, two of Lois Lowery's books won Newbery Medals.

_____ 15. I read her 1990 book, but I can't name the second winner.

_____ 16. It's <u>The Giver</u>, and it won the Newbery Medal in 1994.

Name

Read or listen to the directions. Fill in the circle beside the best answer.

☐ Example:

Which punctuation mark should be at the end of this sentence?

Who was Robert Peary

(A) period

(B) question mark

(C) exclamation mark

(D) comma

Use your time wisely. If a question seems too tough, skip it and come back to it later.

Answer: B because the sentence is an interrogative sentence. It asks a question.

Now try these. You have 20 minutes. Continue until you see .

1. Which sentence should not end with a period?

(A) Robert Peary was an America explorer.

(B) He led eight expeditions to the Arctic.

(C) He attempted to reach the North Pole during the last four expeditions.

(D) Didn't Matthew Henson accompany him.

2. Which name is written correctly?

(A) Ms. Alice R Jenkins

(B) Dr. Laura Young

(C) Rev Wendall Harris

(D) Miss. Maria Thompson

3. Which punctuation mark is used with an abbreviation?

comma	apostrophe	period	question mark
(A)	(B)	(C)	(D)

GO ON ▷

Name

4. Which punctuation mark is used after a capital letter in an outline?

question mark	exclamation mark	comma	period
(A)	(B)	(C)	(D)

5. Which sentence has the correct punctuation mark?

(A) The North Pole lies in the center of the Arctic Ocean!

(B) It is covered with ice!

(C) Sled travel is dangerous here!

(D) Wow, the Arctic Ocean is up to 15,000 feet deep!

6. Which punctuation mark should be used at the end of this sentence?

Robert Peary and Matthew Henson reached the North Pole in 1909

comma	period	question mark	exclamation mark
(A)	(B)	(C)	(D)

7. Which sentence is not punctuated correctly?

(A) Emma was born on November 1, 1990 in Kansas City.

(B) May 17, 1993, is her brother's birthday.

(C) Her mother had another baby on September 9, 1996.

(D) Her parents were both born on April 14, 1960, in Pennsylvania.

8. Which sentence is punctuated correctly?

(A) Are you moving to Garden Hills Illinois next month?

(B) No, my dad decided to take a job in Union, Kentucky, instead.

(C) Say, my grandma lives just across the river in Cincinnati Ohio.

(D) Is that close to Dayton, Ohio or Akron, Ohio?

9. Which greeting of a friendly letter is written correctly?

    (A) Dear Aunt Lucy: (B) Dear Grandma and Grandpa

    (C) Dear Cousin Mike,   (D) Dear Aunt Nancy, and Uncle Ben,

10. Which punctuation mark is needed after the closing of a business letter?

colon	period	comma	NG
(A)	(B)	(C)	(D)

11. In which sentence are the commas used correctly?

    (A) Osgood Perry, and Dexter are three towns in Missouri.

    (B) Osgood, Perry, and Dexter are three towns in Missouri.

    (C) Osgood, Perry and Dexter are three towns in Missouri.

    (D) Osgood, Perry, and Dexter, are three towns in Missouri.

12. Which sentence is written correctly?

    (A) Tim has a list of chores: make his bed feed the cat and rake the leaves.

    (B) Tim has a list of chores make his bed, feed the cat, and rake the leaves.

    (C) Tim has a list of chores, make his bed, feed the cat, and rake the leaves.

    (D) Tim has a list of chores: make his bed, feed the cat, and rake the leaves.

13. Which sentence is not written correctly?

    (A) Daniel, please turn off the television.

    (B) Please turn off the television Daniel.

    (C) Please, Daniel, turn off the television.

    (D) Please turn off the television, Daniel.

GO ON ▷

14. In which sentence is the comma or commas used correctly?

(A) I will, of course, be glad to turn off the TV.

(B) I will of course, be glad to turn off the TV.

(C) I will, of course be glad to turn off the TV.

(D) I will of course be glad to turn off the TV.

15. After which word should a comma be used in this sentence?

Pamela kept looking for her umbrella but she never did find it.

Pamela	looking	but	NG
(A)	(B)	(C)	(D)

16. Which punctuation mark is needed following the word **grumbled**?

Jason grumbled "I'm really tired today."

period	comma	question mark	colon
(A)	(B)	(C)	(D)

17. Which sentence is not written correctly?

(A) "Can you name the longest bridge in America?" asked Emma.

(B) "Is it the Golden Gate Bridge?" answered Liz.

(C) "Emma replied, No it's the Verrazano Narrows Bridge."

(D) "How long is it?" asked Liz.

18. Which sentence is written correctly?

(A) Kelli saw a rerun of "The Aristocats."

(B) She liked the movie, <u>The Princess Diaries</u>, better.

(C) Kelli wants to rent the video of Cats and Dogs.

(C) She liked "Harry Potter and the Sorcerer's Stone the best.

GO ON

19. Which sentence is not punctuated correctly?

(A) Lets all go to Mary's house on Thanksgiving.

(B) Suzy said she'll bring the turkey.

(C) Matt and Dan are going to watch Alex's football game.

(D) We're going to have a lot of fun.

20. Which sentence uses commas correctly?

(A) Santa Fe, the state capital of New Mexico is a great place to visit, Bryan.

(B) Bryan, Santa Fe, the state capital of New Mexico, is a great place to visit.

(C) Santa Fe, the state capital of New Mexico is a great place to visit, Bryan.

(D) Bryan Santa Fe, the state capital of New Mexico, is a great place to visit.

Write the following sentence correctly. List the punctuation rules you used to correct the sentence.

Melanie asked. 'What are you doing after school today.'

_____

_____

_____

_____

Name

Homophones

Homophones are words that are pronounced the same, but are spelled differently and have different meanings. Homophones are often confusing. Example: Juan <u>passed</u> around pictures of stagecoaches from the <u>past</u>. (*Passed* and *past* sound the same, but *passed* is a verb, and *past* is a noun.)

Stagecoach

Complete each sentence with the correct homophone.

1. Stagecoach travel became popular after the United States _____ the Revolutionary War in 1783. (one, won)

2. Benjamin Franklin organized a system to distribute _____ between the new states. (mail, male)

3. Franklin decided that the best _____ to do that was by stagecoach. (way, weigh)

4. Stagecoaches traveled about 10 miles an _____. (hour, our)

5. A _____ could go faster than that, but it could not carry much. (hoarse, horse)

6. Passengers also _____ in stagecoaches. (road, rode)

7. If the trip was long, the driver _____ stop at a wayside inn. (wood, would)

8. Passengers often spent the _____ sleeping on the floor, if the inn was crowded. (knight, night)

9. During the Gold Rush days in California, stagecoaches carried _____ and their gold. (miners, minors)

10. Wells Fargo and Company had armed guards on their coaches, which _____ them safer than other companies' stagecoaches. (made, maid)

11. The company also had detectives who _____ down any bandits who attacked their coaches. (tracked, tract)

12. Wells Fargo used the Central _____ between St. Joseph, Missouri, and San Francisco, California. (Root, Route)

Write a sentence for each pair of these homophones: hall, haul; pause, paws.

Pronoun agreement with antecedents

A **pronoun** is a word that can be used in place of a noun. The noun or noun phrase to which it refers is called its **antecedent**. A pronoun must clearly refer to its antecedent. A pronoun must agree with its antecedent.

Example: Some animals eat only meat. They are called carnivores. (*They* clearly refers to *some animals. Some animals* is a plural subject, so *they* is the correct pronoun to use.)

Sometimes a pronoun replaces other pronouns. You and I are not carnivores. We are omnivores. (*You* and *I* are subject pronouns that can stand alone. *We* refers to *you and I.*)

Practical Pronouns

Subject Pronouns	Object Pronouns	Possessive Pronouns
you, I, he, she, it, we, they	you, me, him, her, it, us, them	my, you, his, her, its, our, your, their, mine, ours, yours, theirs

Complete each sentence with the correct pronoun. Circle its antecedent.

1. Marcus is writing a science report. _____ is about animals that are predators.

2. You and I can learn about these animals, too. _____ can read Marcus's report.

3. Bears eat meat and fish, as well as plant foods. _____ are called omnivores.

4. Sharks use their senses of smell and sight. Sharks use _____ to catch their prey.

5. Some animals use protective camouflage. Green mantises use _____ to catch unsuspecting insects.

6. A Komodo dragon eats pigs and deer. The reptile lashes _____ victims with its powerful tail before biting them.

7. Martens are mammals that must be fearless. _____ prey on porcupines!

8. The secretary bird may seem strange to you and me. Marcus's report tells _____ that this bird first hits a snake with its wings, and then stomps it to death.

9. An electric eel produces electricity. The eel uses _____ to stun its prey.

10. Marcus wrote an interesting report. I hope _____ receives a good grade for it.

Irregular verbs   Unit 7

A past tense verb tells about something that has already happened. Most past tense verbs are formed by adding **-ed** to the present tense verb.

Irregular verbs have their own unique past tense forms.
Example: Granny <u>told</u> me about her pioneer grandmother. (tell)

The present perfect tense tells about something that has happened in the past and is still happening now. It can also tell about something that happened at an indefinite time in the past. Most present perfect tense verbs are formed by using *has* or *have* with the main verb called the past participle.

Irregular verbs have their own unique present perfect forms.
Example: She <u>has told</u> me the story before, but I always like to hear it again. (tell)

Westward, Ho!

Fill in the chart with the correct forms of the irregular verbs. Refer to a dictionary if needed.

Present	Past	Past With Has or Have
1. forgive	_____	has or have _____
2. _____	drove	has or have _____
3. _____	_____	has or have built
4. ring	_____	has or have _____
5. _____	_____	has or have taken

Write the past tense of the irregular verbs in parentheses.

6. The wagon train _____ Independence, Missouri, in May, 1844. (leave)

7. The women _____ with their husbands, hoping to find a better life in Oregon or California. (go)

8. They _____ many hardships to overcome all the way. (find)

9. The pioneers _____ boots and high-topped shoes to protect their feet. (wear)

10. Broad-brimmed hats for the men and sunbonnets for the women _____ them shaded from the harsh summer sun. (keep)

11. The ox-drawn wagons _____ all their possessions. (hold)

12. Sometimes the young children _____ in the crowded covered wagons. (ride)

13. Most of the time, the older ones _____ to walk with their parents. (choose)

14. They _____ friends with other boys and girls in the wagon train. (make)

Name

Irregular verbs

A past tense verb tells about something that has already happened. Most past tense verbs are formed by adding **-ed** to the present tense verb.

Irregular verbs have their own unique past tense forms.
Example: Many birds <u>flew</u> south in autumn. (fly)

The present perfect tense tells about something that has happened in the past and is still happening now. It can also tell about something that happened at an indefinite time in the past. Most present perfect tense verbs are formed by using has or have with the main verb called the past participle.

Irregular verbs have their own unique present perfect forms.
Example: They <u>have flown</u> to the same wintering place year after year. (fly)

Some irregular verbs have the same past and past perfect spellings.
Example: tell, told, have told

A few past and past perfect irregular verbs have the same spellings as the present tense verbs. Example: put, put, has put

Winter in the Woods

Fill in the chart with the correct forms of the irregular verbs. Refer to a dictionary if needed.

Present	Past	Past With Has or Have
1. _____	lost	has or have _____
2. _____	_____	has or have caught
3. _____	_____	has or have known
4. hear	_____	has or have _____

Complete the sentence with the past form of the irregular verb in parentheses.

5. The beaver _____ a winter lodge. (build)

6. The moose _____ a thicker coat for the arrival of colder weather. (grow)

7. The woodchuck _____ a great amount of food before hibernating. (eat)

8. The food _____ fat stored in the woodchuck's body. (become)

Complete the sentence with the present perfect form of the irregular verb in parentheses.

9. The fat _____ down into energy during hibernation. (break)

10. It _____ the woodchuck alive while it was not eating. (keep)

11. As the woodchuck _____, its heartbeat has slowed down. (sleep)

Name

Irregular verbs   Unit 7

Some verbs are easily confused because they are so often misused. Learning their meanings and their various verb forms should help you use them correctly in speaking and writing. Study these pairs of verbs before completing the exercise below.

Teach means to instruct, to inform, or instill knowledge.
Learn means to gain knowledge, to receive instruction, or to comprehend through study.

Lay means to put or set down.
Lie means to be at rest as in a bed or to recline.

Raise means to move to a higher position; to elevate.
Rise means to stand up after lying, sitting, or kneeling; to get out of bed.

Set means to put in a particular place; to arrange for use.
Sit means to rest the body in a sitting position as in a chair.

Easing the Confusion

Complete the chart of verb tenses. Refer to a dictionary if needed.

Present	Past	Present Perfect With Has or Have	Participle
1. _____	_____	_____	teaching
2. learn	_____	_____	_____
3. _____	laid	_____	_____
4. _____	_____	lain	_____
5. raise	_____	_____	_____
6. _____	_____	_____	rising
7. _____	_____	set	_____
8. _____	sat	_____	_____

Underline the correct verb in parentheses to complete each sentence.

9. Joni (lay, laid) in bed and waited for the alarm to go off.

10. She (raised, rose) and put on her clothes for school.

11. Joni hurried downstairs to (sit, set) the table for breakfast.

12. Then she (set, sat) down to review her spelling words.

13. She was (teaching, learning) how to spell tricky homophones.

Subject/verb agreement   Unit 7

The **verb** in the **predicate** of a sentence **must agree** with the **subject** of the sentence.

If the subject is singular, add **–s** or **–es** to most present tense verbs. Remember, if the subject is a collective noun that is used as a unit, it is considered singular. Examples: Our community *has* a rowboat race every Fourth of July. Dad *enters* the race every year.

If the subject of the sentence is plural, the main present tense verb does not change.

Row, Row, Row Your Boat

Choose the verb in parentheses that agrees with the subject of the sentence. Write it in the blank.

1. People _____ various kinds of watercraft for pleasure. (use, uses)

2. Old-fashioned muscle power _____ some types of watercraft. (propel, propels)

3. The first rafts _____ made by tying pieces of wood together. (was, were)

4. Pacific Islanders _____ out tree trunks to make dugout canoes. (digs, dug)

5. The world's largest dugout canoe _____ 70 people. (carry, carries)

6. Boys and girls often _____ canoeing at summer camps. (enjoy, enjoys)

7. One paddler _____ a type of canoe called a kayak. (steer, steers)

8. The paddle _____ double-bladed. (is, are)

9. Rowboats _____ usually heavier and wider than canoes. (is, are)

10. The rower _____ on two oars to steer the boat. (pull, pulls)

11. Rowboats _____ not tip over as easily as canoes. (do, does)

12. Adults and children often _____ from rowboats on lakes and rivers. (fish, fishes)

13. People _____ special lightweight, narrow rowboats called shells. (race, races)

14. Some shells _____ eight racers; others only one. (hold, holds)

15. Teams _____ in races called regattas. (compete, competes)

105 Teach & Test Language: Grade 5

Name _____

Subject/verb agreement   Unit 7

The **verb** in the **predicate** of a sentence **must agree** with the **subject** of the sentence.

If the subject is singular, add **–s** or **–es** to most present tense verbs. Remember, if the subject is a collective noun that is used as a unit, it is considered singular. Examples: A group of rhinoceroses gathers at a water hole. A photographer photographs one of the rhinoceroses.

If the subject of the sentence is plural, the main present tense verb does not change.

Rhinos

Choose the verb that agrees with the subject of each sentence. Write it in the blank.

1. Scientists _____ that rhinoceroses have lived on Earth for about 40 million years.
    (know, knows)

2. Fossils _____ that there were more than 30 species of prehistoric rhinos.
    (show, shows)

3. Rhinoceroses _____ as one of the largest land creatures.
    (rank, ranks)

4. Most wild rhinoceroses _____ in Africa, Southeastern Asia, and Sumatra.
    (live, lives)

5. The five remaining species _____ similar characteristics.
    (share, shares)

6. They _____ horns on their faces, and they _____ huge animals.
    (has, have)   (is, are)

7. Indian rhinos _____ skin that resembles a suit of armor.
    (has, have)

8. A black rhino _____ alone in a place with bushes and trees for protection.
    (live, lives)

9. Indian rhinos _____ marshy jungles among reeds and tall grasses.
    (inhabit, inhabits)

10. A Sumatran rhinoceros _____ unusual because it _____ coarse hair.
    (look, looks)   (has, have)

11. Illegal hunters, called poachers, _____ rhinos for their valuable horns.
    (hunt, hunts)   .

12. Some Africans and Asians _____ up rhino horns to treat sicknesses.
    (grind, grinds)

Name

Combining sentences with nouns and verbs in a series   Unit 7

Combine sentences with related ideas to make one better sentence. You can **combine three or more nouns** in the **subject** or three or more nouns in the **predicate**. Use commas to separate the nouns in a series. Use *and* before the last noun.
Example: Colonial craftspeople made <u>furniture</u>. They made <u>utensils</u>. They made <u>tools</u>. (These sentences have related ideas. Avoid unnecessary repetition by combining the nouns in the predicates.) Colonial craftspeople made <u>furniture</u>, <u>utensils</u>, and <u>tools</u>.

You can **combine three of more verbs** in the **predicate** of a sentence. Use commas to separate the verbs in the series. Use *and* before the last verb.
Example: New apprentices <u>performed simple tasks</u>. They <u>ran errands</u>. They <u>collected payments</u>. (These sentences have related ideas. Avoid unnecessary repetition by combining the verbs in the predicates.) New apprentices <u>performed simple tasks</u>, <u>ran errands</u>, and <u>collected payments</u>.

Colonial Crafts

Read each set of sentences. Combine the nouns or verbs to write a better sentence.

1. Girls in colonial times learned how to spin. They learned how to weave. They learned how to sew. _____

   _____

2. Boys worked for master craftsmen. They learned the necessary skills. They became journeymen. _____

   _____

3. Journeymen traveled the countryside. They made goods. They repaired tools.

   _____

   _____

4. The village blacksmith made iron tools. He made equipment, like pots. He made horseshoes. _____

   _____

5. The gunsmith made the barrel. He made the wooden stock. He made the flintlock used to fire the rifle. _____

   _____

6. Cabinetmakers built furniture. They repaired musical instruments. They built coffins.

   _____

   _____

Combining sentences with adjectives and adverbs Unit 7

More than one **adjective** can describe the same noun. Example: <u>Beautiful</u> *fir trees* grow in California. <u>Green</u> *fir trees* grow in California.

The subjects of the two sentences are the same. The adjectives describe the same nouns. Combine the two sentences to make a better sentence. Use a comma or *and* between the adjectives. Example: <u>Beautiful</u>, <u>green</u> *fir trees* grow in California. <u>Beautiful</u> *and* <u>green</u> *fir trees* grow in California.

More than one adverb can describe the action of the same verb. Example: My brother and I *walked* <u>slowly</u> through the forest. My brother and I *walked* <u>silently</u> through the forest.

The subjects of the two sentences are the same. The adverbs describe the action of the same verb in the predicates. Combine the sentences to make a better sentence. Use *and* between the adverbs. Example: My brother and I *walked* <u>slowly</u> *and* <u>silently</u> through the forest.

Facts About Firs

Read each set of sentences. Combine the adjectives or adverbs to write a better sentence.

1. Fir trees are some of the oldest living things on Earth. Fir trees are some of the tallest living things on Earth. _____

   _____

2. A fir tree's seeds are inside a hard cone. A fir tree's seeds are inside a protective cone. _____

   _____

3. The tree's needles are hard. The needles are narrow and are covered by a waxy layer. _____

   _____

4. Heartwood is the hardest part of the fir tree. Heartwood is the oldest part of the fir tree. _____

   _____

5. The fir's taproot grows straight down. The fir's taproot grows continually.

   _____

6. Water and minerals from the soil flow up. Water and minerals flow out to the needles.

   _____

On another sheet of paper, write a sentence with two adjectives that describe the same noun. Underline the two adjectives.

Name

Combining sentences with appositives

An **appositive** is a word or phrase that explains or identifies a noun. In some instances, you can combine sentences by using information from one to explain or identify a noun in another sentence. Use commas to separate the appositive from the rest of the sentence. The appositive should directly follow the noun.

Example: Goodyear blimps ruled the skies for almost 20 years. The Goodyear Tire and Rubber Company owned them. Goodyear *blimps*, <u>owned by the Goodyear Tire and Rubber Company</u>, ruled the skies for almost 20 years. (The appositive that is underlined identifies the noun in italics in the first sentence.)

Big and Beautiful

Read each pair of sentences. Use information from the second sentence to write an appositive for the underlined noun or phrase in the first sentence. Write the new sentence on the line.

1. There were three <u>blimps</u> in the Goodyear fleet. They were the *Enterprise*, the *Columbia*, and the *America*. _____

_____

2. Each <u>blimp</u> traveled 100,000 miles a year. The blimps were in constant demand.

_____

3. The blimps appeared at major college football <u>games</u>. They were seen at the Orange Bowl and Rose Bowl games. _____

_____

4. They flew high above the <u>Indianapolis 500</u>. The Indianapolis 500 is an auto race.

_____

5. Each <u>blimp</u> cost 5.5 million dollars to build. Each one was 192 feet long. _____

_____

6. It cost a great <u>deal</u> to keep the fleet flying. The cost was 10 million dollars a year.

_____

7. The *Enterprise* had a special <u>feature</u>. It was called the "Super Skytacular."

_____

8. The "<u>Super Skytacular</u>" flashed messages at night to the audience below. It had two electric signs. _____

_____

Name

Using exact nouns, verbs, adjectives, and adverbs   Unit 7

Use **exact nouns** and **verbs** in speaking and writing to make your ideas as clear and precise as possible. Example: An <u>animal</u> <u>goes</u> from limb to limb. (*Animal* and *goes* are not specific words.) A <u>chimpanzee</u> <u>swings</u> from limb to limb. (This sentence is clearer.)

Use **exact adjectives** to describe nouns and express your ideas more clearly. Example: The <u>young</u> *chimpanzee* swings from limb to limb.

Use exact adverbs to describe the action of verbs more clearly. Example: The young chimpanzee *swings* <u>wildly</u> from limb to limb.

Charming Chimps!

Underline the word in parentheses that makes each sentence clearer.

1. Chimpanzees are (nice, sociable) animals, and they are often seen smiling (big, broadly).

2. Chimpanzees live in parts of Africa where jungle (fruit, vegetation) is plentiful.

3. They (hold, grip) tree branches with their long palms and fingers.

4. These (animals, primates) climb trees (well, easily).

5. Chimps have (excellent, good) eyesight, and they are able to see depth and color.

6. They also have a (good, keen) sense of smell that helps them find ripe fruit to eat.

7. Chimpanzees are (bright, intelligent), and they can solve problems.

8. If a chimpanzee wants to eat termites, it (pokes, puts) a twig down into the center of a termite mound.

9. Then it removes the twig and (picks, plucks) off the termites.

10. A male chimpanzee may become (upset, agitated) during a (bad, fierce) rainstorm.

11. He might (run, charge) down a hill, (taking, ripping) off trees branches.

12. He will beat the ground as he (walks, bounds) through the grass.

Write three words for each word that are clearer and more precise words.

13. happy _____ _____ _____

14. say _____ _____ _____

15. person _____ _____ _____

16. well _____ _____ _____

Name

Usage

Read or listen to the directions. Fill in
the circle beside the best answer.

☐ Example:

Which is not true of homophones?

Take time
to review
your
answers.

(A) They are words that have different meanings.

(B) They are words that have the same sounds.

(C) They are words that are spelled the same.

Answer: C because homophones are spelled differently.

Now try these. You have 20 minutes. Continue until you see ⬡STOP .

Which set of words are not homophones?

1.
(A) chose, chews
(B) board, bored
(C) links, lynx
(D) coop, coupe

2.
(A) manners, manors
(B) neigh, nay
(C) clause, caws
(D) side, sighed

---

3. Which sentence does not contain a pair of homophones?

(A) The doctor tried in vane to locate his patient's vein.

(B) We like to hear him sing the hymn.

(C) I'll loan you the money, if you'll leave me alone.

(D) Joel was in a daze for days after winning the lottery.

---

4. Which word is the antecedent of the underlined pronoun?

Mudslides blocked the main highway. They washed away cars and houses.

Mudslides
(A)

blocked
(B)

highway
(C)

cars
(D)

GO ON ▷

---

5. Which pronoun could replace the underlined words in the sentence?

The bumblebee flitted from flower to flower.

He
(A)

She
(B)

It
(C)

They
(D)

6. Which is the correct present perfect tense of the irregular verb **teach**?

will teach
(A)

taught
(B)

has taught
(C)

is teaching
(D)

7. In which sentence is a form of the irregular verb **wear** used correctly?

(A) Shelly wear her raincoat yesterday.

(B) She is wearing it today, also.

(C) Shelly worn it three days in a row.

(D) She has weared it many times.

8. Which sentence has an irregular verb?

(A) Derek moved to San Antonio last week.

(B) He left his baseball mitt at my house.

(C) He called to tell me he needed it.

(D) I will mail it to him today.

Which words are the correct verbs to complete sentences 9 and 10?

9. Emma feels ill, so she is _____ down.

laying
(A)

lying
(B)

lain
(C)

laid
(D)

GO ON

10. Grandmother _____ the vase on the table.

sit	setted	sat	NG
(A)	(B)	(C)	(D)

11. In which sentence does the verb agree with the subject?

(A) People is destroying tropical rain forests.

(B) Public awareness of the problem are increasing.

(C) Some governments promote conservation of rain forests.

(D) Much of the destruction occur in Southeast Asia.

12. In which sentence does the verb not agree with the subject?

(A) Typhoons are cyclones in the Indian Ocean.

(B) Tornadoes damages homes and buildings.

(C) A hurricane often causes flooding.

(D) Hail causes millions of dollars of damage to crops each year.

13. In which sentence does the verb agree with the subject?

(A) Flower spiders eats insects and bees.

(B) They has two large front eyes and good eyesight.

(C) They patiently wait on flowers to grab their prey.

(D) They moves and looks a lot like crabs.

GO ON

14. Which sentence is the correct way to combine the three sentences?

Sirius is a bright star in the northern sky. Procyon is a bright star in the northern sky. Betelgeuse is a bright star in the northern sky.

(A) Sirius is a bright star in the northern sky, and so is Procyon and so is Betelgeuse.

(B) Sirius, Procyon, and Betelgeuse are bright stars in the northern sky.

(C) Sirius and Procyon and Betelgeuse are bright stars in the northern sky.

(D) Sirius and Procyon are bright stars in the northern sky and Betelgeuse.

15. Which sentence is the correct way to combine the three sentences?

A female snapping turtle lays her eggs on land. She packs dirt over them. She returns to the water.

(A) A female snapping turtle lays her eggs on land, packs dirt over them, and returns to the water.

(B) A female snapping turtle lays her eggs on land and packs dirt over them and returns to the water.

(C) A female snapping turtle lays her eggs on land, and she packs dirt over them, and she returns to the water.

(D) A female snapping turtle lays her eggs on land packs dirt over them, and returns to the water.

16. Which sentence is the best way to combine the sentences?

Windsor Castle is the largest castle still used as a home. It is the oldest castle still used as a home.

(A) Windsor Castle is the largest castle and the oldest still used as a home.

(B) Windsor Castle is the largest, oldest castle still used as a home.

(C) Windsor is the largest castle still used as a home, and it is the oldest castle still used as a home.

(D) Windsor Castle is the largest and the castle is the oldest still used as a home.

Unit 7 Test

17. What is combined in the sentence?

Carmen plays the piano beautifully and brilliantly.

adverbs	verbs	adjectives	NG
(A)	(B)	(C)	(D)

18. Which sentence is combined using an appositive?

The fir tree's buds open, and new twigs come out. New twigs are called shoots.

(A) The fir tree's buds open, and new twigs come out, and they are called shoots.

(B) The fir tree's buds open, and new twigs that are called shoots come out.

(C) The fir tree's buds open, and new twigs, called shoots, come out.

(D) The fir tree's buds, shoots, open and new twigs come out.

19. Which sentence contains two exact nouns?

(A) We saw the group of animals.　　(B) We saw a colony of penguins.

(C) We saw a group of penguins.　　(D) We saw a colony of animals.

20. Which sentence contains an exact adjective and an exact adverb?

(A) The baby cried loudly.　　(B) The tiny baby cried.

(C) The tiny baby cried loudly.　　(D) The baby cried now.

Demonstrate how these two sentences can be combined using an appositive.

Lord Cornwallis was taken prisoner at Yorktown. Cornwallis was the British commander.

_____

_____

_____

STOP

Final Review Test Name Grid

Write your name in pencil in the boxes along the top. Begin with your last name. Fill in as many letters as will fit. Then follow the columns straight down and bubble in the letters that correspond with the letters in your name. Complete the rest of the information the same way. You may use a piece of scrap paper to help you keep your place.

STUDENT'S NAME

LAST   FIRST   MI

SCHOOL

TEACHER

FEMALE ○   MALE ○

DATE OF BIRTH

MONTH	DAY	YEAR
JAN ○	⓪ ⓪	⓪ ⓪
FEB ○	① ①	① ①
MAR ○	② ②	② ②
APR ○	③ ③	③ ③
MAY ○	④	④ ④
JUN ○	⑤	⑤ ⑤
JUL ○	⑥	⑥ ⑥
AUG ○	⑦	⑦ ⑦
SEP ○	⑧	⑧ ⑧
OCT ○	⑨	⑨ ⑨
NOV ○		
DEC ○		

GRADE ③ ④ ⑤

(Name grid columns contain bubbles A through Z for each letter position)

Final Review Test Answer Sheet

Pay close attention when transferring your answers. Fill in the bubbles neatly and completely. You may use a piece of scrap paper to help you keep your place.

SAMPLES
A Ⓐ Ⓑ ● Ⓓ
B Ⓕ ● Ⓗ Ⓙ

1 Ⓐ Ⓑ Ⓒ Ⓓ	7 Ⓐ Ⓑ Ⓒ Ⓓ	13 Ⓐ Ⓑ Ⓒ Ⓓ	19 Ⓐ Ⓑ Ⓒ Ⓓ	25 Ⓐ Ⓑ Ⓒ Ⓓ
2 Ⓕ Ⓖ Ⓗ Ⓙ	8 Ⓕ Ⓖ Ⓗ Ⓙ	14 Ⓕ Ⓖ Ⓗ Ⓙ	20 Ⓕ Ⓖ Ⓗ Ⓙ	26 Ⓕ Ⓖ Ⓗ Ⓙ
3 Ⓐ Ⓑ Ⓒ Ⓓ	9 Ⓐ Ⓑ Ⓒ Ⓓ	15 Ⓐ Ⓑ Ⓒ Ⓓ	21 Ⓐ Ⓑ Ⓒ Ⓓ	27 Ⓐ Ⓑ Ⓒ Ⓓ
4 Ⓕ Ⓖ Ⓗ Ⓙ	10 Ⓕ Ⓖ Ⓗ Ⓙ	16 Ⓕ Ⓖ Ⓗ Ⓙ	22 Ⓕ Ⓖ Ⓗ Ⓙ	28 Ⓕ Ⓖ Ⓗ Ⓙ
5 Ⓐ Ⓑ Ⓒ Ⓓ	11 Ⓐ Ⓑ Ⓒ Ⓓ	17 Ⓐ Ⓑ Ⓒ Ⓓ	23 Ⓐ Ⓑ Ⓒ Ⓓ	29 Ⓐ Ⓑ Ⓒ Ⓓ
6 Ⓕ Ⓖ Ⓗ Ⓙ	12 Ⓕ Ⓖ Ⓗ Ⓙ	18 Ⓕ Ⓖ Ⓗ Ⓙ	24 Ⓕ Ⓖ Ⓗ Ⓙ	30 Ⓕ Ⓖ Ⓗ Ⓙ

Name

Read or listen to the directions. Fill in the circle beside the best answer.

☐ Example:

Which word is not a common noun?

(A) conference

(B) convention

(C) assembly

(D) gather

Answer: D because it is a verb.

Now try these. You have 30 minutes.

Continue until you see .

Remember your Helping Hand Strategies:

 1. Cross out answers you know are wrong.

 2. Use your time wisely. If a question seems too tough, skip it and come back to it later.

 3. Take time to review your answers.

 4. Transfer your answers carefully. Use a piece of scratch paper to keep you place on the answer sheet.

---

1. Which word is an abstract noun?

Paul wisely controlled his anger after the accident.

wisely	controlled	anger	accident
(A)	(B)	(C)	(D)

---

2. Which word is not a proper noun?

Thomas Jefferson replaced Benjamin Franklin as ambassador to France.

Jefferson	Franklin	ambassador	France
(F)	(G)	(H)	(J)

---

3. Which word in the sentence is a collective noun?

The audience applauded loudly for the singers and dancers.

audience	applauded	singers	NG
(A)	(B)	(C)	(D)

GO ON >

Name

4. Which line of the outline is written correctly?

   (F) I. Mexican History

   (G) A. The First People in Mexico

   (H) B. the Aztec Empire

   (J) C. war with the United States

5. Which word is not the past tense of an irregular verb?

   caught (A)   heard (B)   worried (C)   began (D)

6. Which word is a present perfect tense verb?

   smile (F)   smiled (G)   is smiling (H)   has smiled (J)

7. Which word is the past progressive tense of **annoy**?

   annoyed (A)   was annoying (B)   annoys (C)   is annoying (D)

8. Which sentence has a contraction?

   (F) Dr. Holt's speech was about solar energy.

   (G) Solar power harnesses the sun's energy.

   (H) It's used for heating homes.

   (J) The walls and floors absorb the day's heat and release it at night.

9. Which word is an adjective in the sentence?

Brenda will clean her disorderly bedroom eventually.

   clean (A)   disorderly (B)   bedroom (C)   eventually (D)

GO ON

Name _____

10. Which is the correct form of the adverb to complete the sentence?

Wally rode his bike _____ down the steep hill.

recklessly	reckless	most recklessly	more recklessly
(F)	(G)	(H)	(J)

11. Which sentence has a double negative?

(A) "Can't you hurry?" asked Bill.

(B) "I don't want no one to be ahead of us in line," he said.

(C) Jerry said, "Well, I won't be too much longer."

(D) "I never like to be late, either," he continued.

12. Which sentence does not have a prepositional phrase?

(F) An atoll is a coral reef.

(G) It is in the shape of a ring.

(H) There may be a lagoon inside the atoll.

(J) It may have cays leading to the ocean.

13. What kind of sentence is this sentence?

Oh no, here comes a swarm of bees!

interrogative	declarative	exclamatory	imperative
(A)	(B)	(C)	(D)

14. Which sentence has the complete subject underlined?

(F) William Dickson built <u>the first reliable movie camera in 1891</u>.

(G) <u>He used different elements</u> from existing machines.

(H) <u>His camera</u> worked by turning a handle.

(J) <u>A sprocket pulled the film</u> through the machine.

GO ON

15. Which sentence is a compound sentence?

(A) Flamingoes are large wading birds, and they have pink feathers.

(B) Flamingoes eat algae and snails.

(C) They eat other tiny aquatic animals.

(D) They hold their bills upside-down in the water.

16. Which sentence has a dependent clause?

(F) The woodpecker finch is an unusual bird.

(G) The bird likes to eat grubs, which are found under tree bark.

(H) It uses a tool to help it get something to eat.

(J) The woodpecker finch sticks a cactus spine under the bark to get to the grubs.

17. Which sentence is not written correctly?

(A) "Do you have Gina's address?" asked Fred.

(B) "Yes, I will give it to you," answered Michelle.

(C) "She lives at 5687 Tucker Avenue" Michelle said.

(D) "Thanks, I want to send her an invitation to my party."

18. Which sentence is not written correctly?

(F) The Mall of America has an indoor roller coaster.

(G) The West Edmonton Mall in Alberta, Canada, has one also.

(H) The Beast is a wooden roller coaster near Cincinnati, Ohio.

(J) It is at Paramount's Kings Island amusement park.

19. Which line of the inside address of a business letter is not written correctly?

(A) Mr. Alfred J. Porter, President

(B) Porter's Popular Pickles

(C) 1632 Grover Street

(D) Greenwood Park New Jersey 08071

20. Which sentence uses capital letters correctly?

(F) The Yangtze River in China is the world's third longest River.

(G) The Great Wall of China was built entirely by hand.

(H) Confucius was a great Chinese Philosopher.

(J) Marco Polo, his Father, and his Uncle traveled to China.

21. In which sentence are commas used correctly?

(A) Lewis and Clark gave Chief Oto fishhooks, tobacco, medals, and army jackets.

(B) Lewis, and Clark, gave Chief Oto fishhooks, tobacco, medals, and army jackets.

(C) Lewis and Clark gave Chief, Oto, fishhooks tobacco medals and army jackets.

(D) Lewis and Clark gave Chief Oto fishhooks, tobacco medals, and army jackets.

22. Which sentence is written correctly?

(F) Limestone, a rock, is made of the limey remains, of sea creatures.

(G) Stalactites and stalagmites, both form in limestone caves.

(H) Cone-shaped formations, stalactites, hang from a cave's roof.

(J) Stalagmites, cone-shaped formations grow upward from the floor.

Final Review Test

23. Which punctuation mark is needed after the word **beach**?

Kara packed four things for the beach a swimsuit, a towel, sunscreen, and a hat.

an apostrophe
(A)

a comma
(B)

a period
(C)

NG
(D)

24. Which sentence does not contain a pair of homophones?

(F) Their father is sitting next to their mother.

(G) It's plain to see that the plane is leaving.

(H) The baker was in tears when the tiers of the cake fell.

(J) It's great to have a grater to grate the cheese.

25. Which word is the antecedent of the underlined pronoun?

The great horned owls eat birds, rabbits, and even skunks. <u>They</u> even swallow fur, bones, and claws.

owls
(A)

rabbits
(B)

skunks
(C)

NG
(D)

26. Which word is the correct verb to complete the sentence?

As soon as Mary _____, we will go to school.

raises
(F)

rises
(G)

risen
(H)

raised
(J)

27. In which sentence does the verb not agree with the subject?

(A) Astronomers studies comets with large telescopes.

(B) A comet's light is reflected sunlight.

(C) Its nucleus is made of ice and gases mixed with dirt.

(D) The head of a comet can be larger than Earth.

GO ON

28. Which sentence is combined using an appositive?

Halley's comet is the most famous comet. It appears once every 76 years.

(F) Halley's comet is the most famous comet, and it appears once every 76 years.

(G) Halley's comet is the most famous comet that appears once every 76 years.

(H) Halley's comet, the most famous comet, appears once every 76 years.

(J) Halley's comet appears once every 76 years.

29. Which part of speech is underlined in the sentence?

Jessie carefully combed her long blond hair <u>before</u> bedtime.

adverb	preposition	conjunction	NG
(A)	(B)	(C)	(D)

30. Which pronoun would complete the sentence correctly?

R.G. and Warren raked up all the leaves by _____.

himself	themselves	yourself	myself
(F)	(G)	(H)	(J)

There is more than one way to combine the three sentences below. Rewrite the sentences to make one better sentence. Explain the method you used to combine them.

Aborigines were the first people to live in Australia. Aborigines had no permanent houses. They constantly moved to find food.

_____

_____

_____

_____

Answer Key

Page 5

Persons: spinster, maiden, infant, orphan, partner, bachelor; Places: pharmacy, mansion, studio, lobby, fortress, university; Things: cabinet, awning, table, hexagon, souvenir, satellite; 1. abstract; 2. abstract; 3. concrete; 4. abstract; 5. abstract; 6. abstract; 7. concrete; 8. abstract

Page 6

1. Soviets, *Sputnik I*; 2. Laika; 3. There are no proper nouns; 4. Yuri Gagarin, Soviet Union; 5. President Kennedy, United States; 6. John Glenn, *Mercury*, Earth; 7. *Apollo 11*; 8. *Columbia*; 9. Neil Armstrong, "Buzz" Aldrin; 10. *Eagle*; 11. White House; 12. New York City; 13. United States; Persons: Soviets, Yuri Gagarin, President Kennedy, John Glenn, Neil Armstrong, "Buzz" Aldrin; Places: Soviet Union, United States, Earth, White House, New York City; Things: *Sputnik I*, Laika, *Mercury*, *Apollo 11*, *Columbia*, *Eagle*

Page 7

1. C; 2. C; 3. C; 4. P; 5. S; 6. S; 7. S; 8. C; 9. C; 10. C; 11. P; 12. C; 13. P; 14. S; 15. C; 16. litter; 17. swarm; 18. gaggle; 19. plague; 20. pod; 21. school; 22. herd; 23. pack; 24.–26. Sentences will vary.

Page 8

1. crashes; 2. comics; 3. ladies; 4. dentists; 5. suggestions; 6. decisions; 7. addresses; 8. branches; 9. glimpses; 10. responsibilities; 11. buzzes; 12. taxes; 13. princesses; 14. displays; 15. tortillas; 16. melodies; 17. mysteries; 18. statues; 19. figures; 20. islanders; 21. eyes; 22. earlobes; 23. monuments; 24. bodies

Page 9

1. sheep; 2. loaves; 3. knives; 4. lives; 5. oxen; 6. mice; 7. echoes; 8. rodeos; 9. leaves; 10. beliefs; 11. teeth; 12. halves; 13. wolves; 14. tomatoes; 15. volcanoes; 16. pianos; 17. thieves; 18. women; 19. cameos; 20. photos; 21. men; 22. safes

Page 10

1. berries'; 2. teeth's; 3. bracelet's; 4. galaxy's; 5. men's; 6. T-rex's; 7. Tess's; 8. children's; 9. industries'; 10. sausages'; 11. meadow's; 12. tennis's; 13. Tuesday's; 14. countesses'; 15. Howard's; 16. melon's; 17. French fries' flavor; 18. Canada's economy; 19. the crowd's cheers; 20. the pies' aroma; 21. the museum's displays; 22. the astronauts' flight; 23. the artist's creations; 24. the immigrants' dreams

Page 11

1. they; 2. they; 3. he; 4. it; 5. we; 6. she; 7. They; 8. He; 9. They; 10. It; 11. They; 12. She; 13. He; 14. They

Page 12

1. it; 2. them; 3. us; 4. it; 5. them; 6. them; 7. them; 8. it; 9. it; 10. them; 11. it; 12. them; 13. him; 14. it; 15. them; 16. him; 17. us

Page 13

1. He; 2. them; 3. She; 4. it; 5. it, her; 6. He, she; 7. He, her; 8. him, her

Page 14

1. Its; 2. their; 3. His; 4. Mine; 5. its; 6. his; 7. its; 8. yours; 9. Mine

Page 15

1. herself; 2. themselves; 3. myself; 4. himself; 5. yourself; 6. himself; 7. itself; 8. themselves; 9. itself; 10. ourselves

Page 16

1. This; 2. Those; 3. What; 4. These; 5. What; 6. That; 7. Who; 8. What; 9. Those; 10. Which

Unit 1 Test

1. C; 2. D; 3. D; 4. B; 5. C; 6. B; 7. A; 8. D; 9. D; 10. A; 11. D; 12. B; 13. D; 14. A; 15. B; 16. C; 17. C; 18. B; 19. C; 20. B; Constructed-response answers will vary.

Page 21

1. yes; 2. yes; 3. yes; 4. yes; 5. no; 6. no; 7. yes; 8. yes; 9. yes; 10. yes; 11. no; 12. no; 13. no; 14. yes; 15. yes; 16. no; 17. yes; 18. yes; 19. yes; 20. yes; 21. float; 21. hatches; 23. hides; 24. protect; 25. swims; 26. searches; 27. eat; 28. use; 29. swallow; 30. scavenge

Page 22

1. L; 2. N; 3. A; 4. A; 5. L; 6. A; 7. A; 8. N; 9. A; 10. L; 11. begins; 12. sell; 13. gather; 14. explodes; 15. shoot; 16. dash; 17. rain; 18. escape; 19. are; 20. cover

Page 23

1. delayed; 2. helped; 3. placed; 4. arrived; 5. slipped; 6. trimmed; 7. magnified; 8. propelled; 9. answered; 10. wanted; 11. applied; 12. carried; 13. supplied; 14. passed; 15. stretched; 16. delivered

Page 24

1. had, L; 2. rotated, A; 3. were, L; 4. had, L; 5. helped, A; 6. wrapped, A; 7. waited, A; 8. spotted, A; 9. exploded, A; 10. struggled, A; 11. pulled, A; 12. chewed, A; 13. had; 14. reflected; 15. was; 16. showed; 17. changed

Page 25

1. hurried, will hurry; 2. browse, browsed; 3. argue, will argue; 4. lectured, will lecture; 5. criticize, will criticize; 6. promote, promoted; 7. past; 8. past; 9. past; 10. past; 11. present; 12. present; 13. present; 14. future; 15. present; 16. future

Page 26

1. have learned; 2. has earned; 3. have studied; 4. have performed; 5. have constructed; 6. are watching; 7. were watching; 8. are changing; 9. were changing; 10. is turning; 11. was turning

Answer Key

Page 27

1. has started; 2. have burned;
3. have ignited; 4. have picked;
5. has moved; 6. is consuming;
7. was consuming; 8. are leaping;
9. were leaping; 10. are shooting;
11. were shooting

Page 28

1. drew, drawn; 2. swim, swum;
3. teach, taught; 4. stood; 5. fell;
6. saw; 7. rose; 8. hid; 9. have
thought; 10. have known; 11. have
chosen; 12. have begun; 13. have
made

Page 29

1. should not; 2. they will; 3. I would;
4. you are; 5. what is or what has;
6. had not; 7. could not; 8. Sherri is;
9. wasn't; 10. they'd; 11. he'll;
12. that's; 13. you've; 14. they've;
15. where's; 16. he's; 17. aren't;
18. can't; 19. She's; 20. They're;
21. doesn't, that's, she'll

Unit 2 Test

1. A; 2. D; 3. C; 4. A; 5. B; 6. A; 7. B;
8. A; 9. D; 10. A; 11. A; 12. B; 13. A;
14. D; 15. A; 16. C; 17. A; 18. A; 19. D;
20. A; Constructed-response: present
perfect, Answers will vary.

Page 35

1. thrilling; 2. watertight; 3. two-
bladed; 4. protective; 5. life; 6. icy,
mountain; 7. raging; 8. jagged;
9. swift, treacherous;
10. experienced; 11. adjective =
Fiberglass, noun = kayaks;
12. adjective = original, noun =
shape; 13. adjective = Wooden, noun
= boats; 14. underline; 15. underline;
16. underline; 17. no underline;
18. no underline; 19. underline;
20. underline; 21. underline;
22. underline; 23. underline;
24. underline, 25 underline

Page 36

1. skinnier, skinniest; 2. lighter,
lightest; 3. more terrible, most terrible;
4. more exceptional, most
exceptional; 5. flimsier, flimsiest;
6. whiter, whitest; 7. more desirable,
most desirable; 8. thinner, thinnest;
9. more responsible; 10. messiest;
11. more trustworthy

Page 37

1. 1; 2. 2; 3. 3; 4. 2; 5. 3; 6. 2; 7. 2;
8. 1; 9. 2; 10. 3

Page 38

1. an; 2. a; 3. a; 4. an; 5. the; 6. the;
7. a; 8. an; 9. an; 10. the; 11. the;
12. the; 13. a; 14. a; 15. a; 16. the;
17. a; 18. an; 19. a; 20. an; 21. an;
22. a; 23. a; 24. a; 25. an; 26. a

Page 39

1. down; 2. there; 3. carefully;
4. nearby; 5. around; 6. Then, deep;
7. rapidly; 8. again; 9. eagerly, up;
10. gently; 11. away; 12. tomorrow;
Adverbs That Tell How: carefully,
rapidly, eagerly, gently; Adverbs That
Tell When: Then, again, tomorrow;
Adverbs That Tell Where: down,
there, nearby, around, deep, up, away

Page 40

1. more completely, most completely;
2. more fondly, most fondly;
3. nearer, nearest; 4. more wearily,
most wearily; 5. closer, closest;
6. more brilliantly, most brilliantly;
7. more timely, most timely; 8. more
seriously, most seriously; 9. more
successfully; 10. more often;
11. truthfully; 12. gladly; 13. handily

Page 41

1. isn't, no, a; 2. never, no, any; 3. No
one, never, ever; 4. Nowhere,
nothing, anything; 5. never, no, any;
6. Haven't, never, ever; 7. wouldn't,
no, any

Page 42

Words in bold should be circled: 1. in,
1850's; 2. above, **trees**; 3. up, **river**;
4. between, **rows**; 5. by, **sandbars**;
6. on, **route**; 7. around, **bend**; 8. for,
day; 9. at, **controls**; 10. under,
branch; 11. in, **1807**; 12. on, **Hudson
River**, in, **New York**; 13. In, **1811**,
from, **Louisville**, **Kentucky**; 14. of,
New Orleans; 15. through, **rapids**,
on, **Ohio River**; 16. of, **Mississippi
River**; 17. of, **surroundings**; 18. in,
canoes; 19. at, **end**, of, **Mississippi**;
20. for, **steamboat**, through,
Mississippi

Page 43

Words in bold should be circled:
1. off, **coast**, of, **Ecuador, South
America**; 2. in, **Pacific Ocean**, in,
beginning; 3. on, **rocks**, on, **islands**,
at, **first**; 4. to, **islands**, on, **winds**;
5. of, **life**, for, **animals**; 6. on, **shores**;
7. from, **mainland**; 8. to, **iguanas**;
9. in, **craters**, of, **volcanoes**; 10. on,
bodies, of, **animals**; 11. on, **blood**,
of, **birds**; 12. among, **rocks**, on,
islands; 13. from, **islands**, to, **coast**,
of, **South America**; 14. in, **1959**;
15. on, **islands**; 16. of, **islands**

Page 44

1. Oh my; 2. Oh boy; 3. Say; 4. Good
grief; 5. Well; 6. Oh; 7. Hey; 8. Phew;
9.–14. Interjections may vary.
9. Hey!; 10. Wow!; 11. Well;
12. Ouch!; 13. Say,; 14. My, oh, my!

Page 45

1. sentences; 2. sentences;
3. sentences; 4. words; 5. words;
6. words; 7. subjects; 8. predicates

Unit 3 Test

1. A; 2. B; 3. C; 4. A; 5. C; 6. B; 7. A;
8. A; 9. D; 10. A; 11. A; 12. D; 13. C;
14. B; 15. A; 16. A; 17. D; 18. A;
19. D; 20. C; Constructed-response
Answers will vary.

Page 51

1. D,.; 2. INT, ?; 3. D, .; 4. IMP, .;
5. INT, ?; 6. D, .; 7. INT, ?; 8. D, .; 9. E,
!; 10. INT, ?; 11. E, !; 12. D, .

Answer Key

Page 52
1. D; 2. I; 3. D; 4. I; 5. D; 6. D; 7. D; 8. I; 9. D; 10. I; 11. D; 12. I; 13. I

Page 53
1. I, ?; 2. E, !; 3. I, ?; 4. E, !; 5. I, ?; 6. I, ?; 7. I, ?; 8. E, !; 9. E, !; 10. I, ?; 11. I, ?; 12. E, !

Page 54
1. D; 2. F; 3. D; 4. R; 5. D; 6. D; 7. R; 8. D; 9. D; 10. D; 11. F; 12. R

Page 55
1. SS = father, SP = hoisted; 2. SS = They, SP = stood; 3. SS = immigrants, SP = had traveled; 4. SS = passengers, SP = wanted; 5. SS = It, SP = was; 6. SS = crowd, SP = cheered; 7. SS = Tears, SP = ran; 8. SS = people, SP = saw; 9. SS = buildings, SP = rose; 10. SS = newcomers, SP = transferred; 11. SS = barges, SP = carried; 12. SS = Ellis Island, SP = was; 13. SS = people, SP = passed; 14. SS = years, SP = were; 15. SS = National Park Service, SP = operates; 16. SS = exhibits, SP = include

Page 56
Words in bold should be circled:
1. CS = A young **girl**, CP = **walks** carefully along the rocky shore.; 2. CS = **Carmen**, CP = **notices** the tide going out.; 3. CS = **Pools** of water, CP = **collect** in rocky crevices along the shore. ; 4. CS = Tide **pools**, CP = **are** home to sea plants and animals.; 5. CS = **Seaweeds**, CP = **are** the most common tide pool plants.; 6. CS = **They**, CP = **provide** food and shelter for a variety of animals.; 7. CS = **Carmen**, CP = **watches** a sea urchin attached to a rock.; 8. CS = **Sea urchins**, CP = **are** little spiny animals with tiny tube feet.; 9. CS = Their **mouths**, CP = **are** on their undersides.; 10. CS = Their sharp **teeth**, CP = **cut** seaweed into little pieces.; 11. CS = **Carmen**, CP = **spies** abalone at another tide pool.; 12. CS = This **mollusk**, CP = **clings** to a rock as it munches kelp.; 13. CS = **Carmen**, CP = **sees** many barnacles attached to the tide pool rocks.; 14. CS = **Barnacles**, CP = **close** their shells during low tide.;

15. CS = These **crustaceans**, CP = **wait** for feeding time at high tide.; 16. CS = **Carmen**, CP = **watches** as the tide creeps back up the beach.

Page 57
1. CP, planting, raising; 2. CS, Chinese, Japanese; 3. N; 4. CS, Fish, shellfish; 5. CS, Overfishing, pollution; 6. CS, Sea farming, ranching; 7. CP, raise, sell; 8. CP, grow, taste; 9. CS, Tuna, salmon; 10. N

Page 58
1. The first saber-toothed cats lived 40 million years ago, and they became extinct about 10,000 years ago.; 2. Saber-toothed tigers had large canine teeth, and the 8-inch teeth were curved like swords.; 3. They were carnivores, and they ate thick-skinned animals like elephants and mastodons.; 4. Prehistoric bears belonged to the carnivora family, but bears were also herbivores.; 5. Mastodons were related to elephant-like animals, but they were stockier and not as tall as elephants and mammoths.

Page 59
1. IC: 2. X; 3. X; 4. IC: 5. X; 6. X; 7. which were called chinampas; 8. Because they did not have cattle; 9. which was their main crop; 10. that sat on three stones; 11. which was called atole; 12. that were sometimes stuffed with snails or boiled grasshoppers

Unit 4 Test
1. C; 2. B; 3. B; 4. B; 5. D; 6. D; 7. B; 8. A; 9. D; 10. D; 11. B; 12. A; 13. B; 14. A; 15. B; 16. D; 17. D; 18. C; 19. A; 20. A; Constructed-response: Answers will vary.

Midway Review Test
1. C; 2. G; 3. D; 4. G; 5. A; 6. G; 7. D; 8. G; 9. A; 10. G; 11. C; 12. J; 13. C; 14. J; 15. B; 16. G; 17. C; 18. J; 19. B; 20. J; Constructed-response: Answers will vary.

Page 71
1. yes; 2. no; 3. no; 4. yes; 5. yes; 6. yes; 7. no; 8. yes; 9. Automobiles; 10. I; 11. Yes; 12. Erupting; 13. Weather; 14. Britain's; 15. Trees

Page 72
1. no; 2. no; 3. yes; 4. yes; 5. yes; 6. yes; 7. no; 8. yes; 9. Betty and Brett Breeze; 10. Carl Edward Smith; 11. Uncle Richard; 12. Grandmother Rebecca; 13. Collin O'Keffe; 14. Auntie Louise; 15. Uncle Marvin, Aunt Susan; 16. Albert, Barry, Sammie; 17. Grandma's, Grandpa's

Page 73
1. Dr. Ronald J. Lohmar; 2. Ms. S. P. Steed; 4. Miss Stacy Justus; 4. Mr. and Mrs. Garcia; 6. Rosa Parks; 6. Ms. Parks; 7. Ms. Jo Ann Robinson, Mr. E. D. Nixon; 8. Dwight D. Eisenhower

Page 74
1. 2148 Serena Pl., Oakland, CA 94601; 2. 5234 Autumn Avenue, Bristol, NY 14469; 3. 17591 Liberty Trail Dr., Deer Park, Illinois 60010; 4. 8820 E. Pacific St., Stony Ridge, Indiana 46538; 5. 4224 Brookstone Terrace, Wildwood, KY 40223; 6. 94 Sun Lake St., Bruin, Pennsylvania 16022; 7. Atlanta, Georgia, Rock Creek, Maryland; 8. Miller Forest Road, Summit City, Michigan; 9. Carriage Crossing Lane; 10. Florence, Nebraska, Fort Morgan, Colorado

Page 75
1. England, Multicultural Week, Bingham School; 2. Tower of London; 3. Buckingham Palace, Westminster Abbey; 4. Northern Ireland, Scotland, Wales, England, United Kingdom; 5. Smithsonian Institution, Washington, D. C., Wednesday; 6. New York Philharmonic Concert, April; 7. Christmas Eve, Hanukkah, Monday

Answer Key

Page 76

Friendly Letter: 6844 Lone Elk Lane, Fox Lake, Minnesota 56181, August 1, 2001, Dear Grandma and Grandpa, Dad and I, We, We, Love, Brenda; Business Letter: 1798 Florence Street, Sunny Slopes, Indiana 47401, February 20, 2002, Ms. Roberta Jones, President, Simply Seeds, Inc., Box 77, Baldwin, Georgia 30511, Dear Ms. Jones:, Please, I, Sincerely, Albert Armstrong, Albert Armstrong

Page 77

I. In New England; A. Protested; B. Elected; C. Defended; II. National Politics; A. Massachusetts; B. Persuaded; C. Served; D. A; E. Wrote

Page 78

1. Julie of the Wolves; 2. Little House on the Prairie; 3. Scientific American Explorations; 4. National Geographic; 5. "The Happy Thought"; 6. "Flower Spiders"; 7. "You're a Grand Old Flag"; 8. "Little One-Inch"; 9. "A Bug's Life"; 10. "Angela Anaconda"

Unit 5 Test

1. D; 2. C; 3. A; 4. D; 5. C; 6. A; 7. C; 8. C; 9. A; 10. D; 11. C; 12. C; 13. A; 14. C; 15. B; 16. D; 17. C; 18. B; 19. B; 20. D; Constructed-response: Answers will vary.

Page 84

1. C, .; 2. D, .; 3. I, .; 4. C, .; 5. D, .; 6. I, .; 7. D, .; 8. C, .; 9. D, .; 10. D, .; 11.–14. Students add periods to each sentence.

Page 85

1. Ms. Paula Shannon; 2. Mr. John W. Weiler; 3. Miss Barbara J. Rizzo; 4. Rev. and Mrs. Handley; 5. Mrs. R. S. Streeter; 6. Dr. Thomas L. Hutson; 7. Patrick Markham, Sr.; 8. Mr. and Mrs. Storey; 9. St.; 10. Thurs.; 11. Jr.; 12. Dec.; 13. Ave.; 14. Dr.; 15. Rev.; 16. Dr.; Aug.; Mr., H., Ms., Dr., Wed., Sept.

Page 86

I., A., B., C.; II., A., B., C., D.; III., A., B.

Page 87

1. I, ?; 2. I, ?; 3. E, !; 4. I, ?; 5. E, !; 6. E, !; 7. I, ?; 8. E, !; 9. E, !; 10. I, ?; 11. ?; 12. ?; 13. !; 14. !; 15. ?

Page 88

1. North Oaks, California; 2. Halawa Hills, HA; 3. December 21, 2000; 4. Dear Uncle Harvey,; 5. Your cousin,; 6. July 18, 2001; 7. Colony Park, Georgia; 8. Dear Mom and Dad,; Magnolia Springs, Maryland; February 3, 2001; Dear Ronnie,; Wednesday, February 8; Canton, Ohio,; Your friend,

Page 89

1. yes; 2. no; 3. yes; 4. yes; 5. no; 6. Some of the earliest jungle films are as follows: "Tarzan the Ape Man," "King Kong," and "Tarzan and His Mate."; 7. "Animal Crackers," "Monkey Business," and "Horse Feathers" were made by the Marx Brothers in the 1930's.; 8. Harpo, Chico, and Groucho Marx made many more silly slapstick films.; 9. Older generations will remember these Jerry Lewis' films: "The Bellboy," "The Nutty Professor," and "The Disorderly Orderly."

Page 90

1. Please tell me more about the Gateway Arch, Mrs. Fowler.; 2. Well, it is made of stainless steel.; 3. The legs are hollow so, consequently, small elevators can go up to the top.; 4. The Arch is in St. Louis on the Mississippi River, Tamika.; 5. Mrs. Fowler, isn't the San Jacinto Monument the tallest column in the world?; 6. Yes, you are correct, Tamika.; 7. The column is 571 feet tall, class, and it has a 220-ton star on top.; 8. Goodness, that must be an impressive sight to see.; 9. Yes, particularly when you consider it was built in 1936.; 10. Show the class this picture of the column, Tamika.; 11. Children, has anyone visited Mount Rushmore in South Dakota?; 12. Currently, Mount Rushmore is the largest completed sculpture in the world.; 13. However, a 564-foot statue is being carved that will be taller than Mount Rushmore.; 14. It is a statue of Chief Crazy Horse, students.

Page 91

1. The Arkansas River flows through a deep canyon, the Royal Gorge, in Colorado.; 2. It flows through Tulsa, the largest city on the river, before reaching Little Rock.; 3. The Colorado River, the longest river west of the Rocky Mountains, empties into the Gulf of California.; 4. The Colorado River has cut deep canyons into rock, and one of these canyons is the Grand Canyon.; 5. The Grand Canyon is 277 miles long, and it is more than a mile deep.; 6. Hoover Dam, the largest dam on the Colorado, is on the border of Arizona and Nevada.; 7. The word "Mississippi," an Algonquian Indian word, means "father of waters.";
8. The Mississippi, a 2,340-mile-long river, is truly the "father of waters.";
9. It is the main river drainage system in America, and it drains an area of 1.2 million square miles.; 10. The country's longest river, the Missouri, is called "The Big Muddy" because it carries so much sediment.

Page 92

1. Tony asked, "What constellation do you see?"; 2. "I see Orion, which is a winter constellation," answered the astronomer.; 3. Dr. Tan continued, "That means it is visible only from late October until April."; 4. "Orion has more bright stars than other constellations," explained Dr. Tan.; 5. The astronomer said, "Here, Tony, look through the telescope."; 6. "Can you find the three bright stars in a row?" asked Dr. Tan.; 7. "Those stars represent Orion's belt, and the dimmer ones are his shield," he said.

Answer Key

Page 93

1. "The King of the Mountain";
2. "The Mice That Ate Iron"; 3. "Home on the Range"; 4. "Give My Regards to Broadway"; 5. "Rebirth of an Urban Prairie"; 6. "End of the Line"; 7. "Hercules"; 8. "Free Willy"; 9. "Loveliest of Trees"; 10. "There Will Come Soft Rains"; 11. "Kids from Room 402"; 12. "Family Matters"

Page 94

1. he'd; 2. won't; 3. shouldn't; 4. they'll; 5. story's; 6. Harriet's; 7. Richard Peek's book; 8. Donald Small's illustrations; 9. Abraham Lincoln's biography; 10. PN; 11. C; 12. PN; 13. PN; 14. PN; 15. C; 16. C

Unit 6 Test

1. D; 2. B; 3. C; 4. D; 5. D; 6. B; 7. A; 8. B; 9. C; 10. C; 11. B; 12. D; 13. B; 14. A; 15. D; 16. B; 17. C; 18. A; 19. A; 20. B; Constructed response: Melanie asked, "What are you doing after school today?"; Answers will vary.

Page 100

1. won; 2. mail; 3. way; 4. hour; 5. horse; 6. rode; 7. would; 8. night; 9. miners; 10. made; 11. tracked; 12. Route

Page 101

1. science report, It; 2. You and I, We; 3. Bears, They; 4. senses of smell and sight, them; 5. protective camouflage, it; 6. Komodo dragon, its; 7. Martens, They; 8. you and me, us; 9. electricity, it; 10. Marcus, he

Page 102

1. forgave, forgiven; 2. drive, driven; 3. build, built; 4. rang, rung; 5. take, took; 6. left; 7. went; 8. found; 9. wore; 10. kept; 11. held; 12. rode; 13. chose; 14. made

Page 103

1. lose, lost; 2. catch, caught; 3. know, knew; 4. heard, heard; 5. built; 6. grew; 7. ate; 8. became; 9. has broken; 10. has kept; 11. has slept

Page 104

1. teach, taught, taught; 2. learned, learned, learning; 3. lay, laid, laying; 4. lie, lay, lying; 5. raised, have raised, raising; 6. rise, rose, risen; 7. set, set, setting; 8. sit, sat, sitting; 9. lay; 10. rose; 11. set; 12. sat; 13. learning

Page 105

1. use; 2. propels; 3. were; 4. dug; 5. carries; 6. enjoy; 7. steers; 8. is; 9. are; 10. pulls; 11. do; 12. fish; 13. race; 14. hold; 15. compete

Page 106

1. know; 2. show; 3. rank; 4. live; 5. share; 6. have, are; 7. have; 8. lives; 9. inhabit; 10. looks, has; 11. hunt; 12. grind

Page 107

1. Girls in colonial times learned how to spin, weave, and sew.; 2. Boys worked for master craftsmen, learned the necessary skills, and became journeymen.; 3. Journeymen traveled the countryside, made goods, and repaired tools.; 4. The village blacksmith made iron tools, equipment, like pots, and horseshoes.; 5. The gunsmith made the barrel, the wooden stock, and the flintlock used to fire the rifle.; 6. Cabinetmakers built furniture, repaired musical instruments, and built coffins.

Page 108

1. Fir trees are some of the oldest and tallest living things on Earth.; 2. A fir tree's seeds are inside a hard, protective cone.; 3. The tree's needles are hard, narrow, and covered by a waxy layer.; 4. Heartwood is the hardest and oldest part of the fir tree.; 5. The fir's taproot grows straight down and continually.; 6. Water and minerals from the soil flow up and out to the needles.

Page 109

1. There were three blimps, the *Enterprise*, the *Columbia*, and the *America*, in the Goodyear fleet.; 2. Each blimp, in constant demand, traveled 100,000 miles a year.; 3. The blimps appeared at major college football games, the Orange Bowl and the Rose Bowl.; 4. They flew high above the Indianapolis 500, an auto race.; 5. Each blimp, 192 feet long, cost 5.5 million dollars to build.; 6. It cost a great deal, 10 million dollars a year, to keep the fleet flying.; 7. The *Enterprise* had a special feature, the "Super Skytacular."; 8. The "Super Skytacular," with two electric signs, flashed messages at night to the audience below.

Page 110

1. sociable, broadly; 2. vegetation; 3. grip; 4. primates, easily; 5. excellent; 6. keen; 7. intelligent; 8. pokes; 9. plucks; 10. agitated, fierce; 11. charge, ripping; 12. bounds; 13.–16. Answers will vary.

Unit 7 Test

1. A; 2. C; 3. C; 4. A; 5. C; 6. C; 7. B; 8. B; 9. B; 10. D; 11. C; 12. B; 13. C; 14. B; 15. A; 16. B; 17. A; 18. C; 19. B; 20. C; Constructed response: Lord Cornwallis, the British commander, was taken prisoner at Yorktown.

Final Review Test

1. C; 2. H; 3. A; 4. F; 5. C; 6. J; 7. B; 8. H; 9. B; 10. F; 11. B; 12. F; 13. C; 14. H; 15. A; 16. G; 17. C; 18. J; 19. D; 20. G; 21. A; 22. H; 23. D; 24. F; 25. A; 26. G; 27. A; 28. H; 29. B; 30. G; Constructed-response: Answer may vary. Sample answer: Aborigines were the first people to live in Australia, had no permanent houses, and constantly moved to find food.